THE NATIONAL ACADEMIES

National Academy of Sciences
National Academy of Engineering
Institute of Medicine
National Research Council

The **National Academy of Sciences** is a private, nonprofit, self-perpetuating society of distinguished scholars engaged in scientific and engineering research, dedicated to the furtherance of science and technology and to their use for the general welfare. Upon the authority of the charter granted to it by the Congress in 1863, the Academy has a mandate that requires it to advise the federal government on scientific and technical matters. Dr. Bruce M. Alberts is president of the National Academy of Sciences.

The **National Academy of Engineering** was established in 1964, under the charter of the National Academy of Sciences, as a parallel organization of outstanding engineers. It is autonomous in its administration and in the selection of its members, sharing with the National Academy of Sciences the responsibility for advising the federal government. The National Academy of Engineering also sponsors engineering programs aimed at meeting national needs, encourages education and research, and recognizes the superior achievements of engineers. Dr. William A. Wulf is president of the National Academy of Engineering.

The **Institute of Medicine** was established in 1970 by the National Academy of Sciences to secure the services of eminent members of appropriate professions in the examination of policy matters pertaining to the health of the public. The Institute acts under the responsibility given to the National Academy of Sciences by its congressional charter to be an adviser to the federal government and, upon its own initiative, to identify issues of medical care, research, and education. Dr. Kenneth I. Shine is president of the Institute of Medicine.

The **National Research Council** was organized by the National Academy of Sciences in 1916 to associate the broad community of science and technology with the Academy's purposes of furthering knowledge and advising the federal government. Functioning in accordance with general policies determined by the Academy, the Council has become the principal operating agency of both the National Academy of Sciences and the National Academy of Engineering in providing services to the government, the public, and the scientific and engineering communities. The Council is administered jointly by both Academies and the Institute of Medicine. Dr. Bruce M. Alberts and Dr. William A. Wulf are chairman and vice chairman, respectively, of the National Research Council.

D1511408

SYMPOSIUM STEERING COMMITTEE

MARYE ANNE FOX, *Chair*, North Carolina State University
MARGARET BURBIDGE, University of California, San Diego
MILDRED COHN, University of Pennsylvania School of Medicine
MILDRED DRESSELHAUS, Massachusetts Institute of Technology (on leave from August 2000)
MARIA NEW, Cornell University Medical College
VERA RUBIN, Carnegie Institute of Washington
KAREN UHLENBECK, University of Texas, Austin
HOWARD GEORGI, Harvard University
LILIAN WU, IBM Corporation

COMMITTEE ON WOMEN IN SCIENCE AND ENGINEERING (1999)

HOWARD GEORGI, *Co-chair*, Harvard University
LILIAN SHIAO-YEN WU, *Co-chair,* IBM Corporation
WILLIE PEARSON JR., Wake Forest University
SUSAN SOLOMON, National Oceanic and Atmospheric Administration (NOAA)
JULIA WEERTMAN, Northwestern University

OSEP ADVISORY BOARD LIAISON

STEPHEN LUKASIK, Independent Consultant

Staff

JONG-ON HAHM, Director
SHIREL SMITH, Project Coordinator

OFFICE OF SCIENTIFIC AND ENGINEERING PERSONNEL ADVISORY COMMITTEE (1999)

M.R.C. GREENWOOD, *Chair,* University of California, Santa Cruz
DAVID BRENEMAN, University of Virginia
CARLOS GUTIERREZ, California State University, Los Angeles
STEPHEN J. LUKASIK, Independent Consultant, Los Angeles
JANET NORWOOD, The Urban Institute
JOHN D. WILEY, University of Wisconsin, Madison
TADATAKA YAMADA, Smith Kline Beecham Corporation
A. THOMAS YOUNG, North Potomac, Maryland
WILLIAM H. MILLER, *ex-officio,* University of California, Berkeley

Staff

CHARLOTTE V. KUH, Executive Director
MARILYN J. BAKER, Associate Executive Director
NINA KAULL, Administrative Officer
CATHY JACKSON, Administrative Associate
EDVIN HERNANDEZ, Administrative Assistant

Preface

Modern science is a complex web of many different people and institutions. If we are to maintain the pace of scientific discovery for the benefit of humankind, scientists need to ensure that outstanding people with many different talents will continue to join the scientific community. Increasingly, we must compete with other communities for the best minds the world has to offer. If science is to continue to prosper and move forward, we must ensure that no source of scientific intellect is overlooked or lost. This means including women and ethnic minorities as active participants in the scientific enterprise.

In 1998, the National Academy of Sciences (NAS) asked the National Research Council's (NRC) Committee on Women in Science and Engineering (CWSE) to host a discussion centered on the challenges facing all scientists in the current scientific climate, but focused particularly on the challenges that women face at every transition point in their careers.

Meeting participants agreed that these challenges contribute to the sharp losses in numbers of women scientists at each career stage, and that the NAS should make a strong statement to focus attention on the importance of enabling women to contribute to and lead in the scientific process. This symposium is the outcome of the 1998 meeting.

The symposium was held during the 1999 NAS annual meeting to address the question, "Who will do the science of the future?" The symposium focused on the need to bring in many viewpoints to science and ways to increase the variety of viewpoints by recruiting and retaining women in science. The speakers, all leaders in their fields, emphasized the need to engage and sustain the interest of women in science, and presented ways in which different institutions have developed approaches to retain women in scientific careers.

The Committee on Women in Science and Engineering was honored to be asked to organize the NAS symposium. Since its inception in 1991 as a standing committee of the NRC, CWSE has worked to coordinate, monitor, and advocate national action on increasing the numbers of women in science and engineering. The committee members represent diverse scientific and engineering disciplines, and all have brought attention to the importance of including women in their own fields.

We would like to thank the staff of CWSE, Dr. Jong-on Hahm, Director, and Shirel Smith, Project Coordinator, for bringing to fruition the ideas of the symposium steering committee and CWSE. We would also like to thank Dr. Charlotte Kuh, Executive Director of the Office of Scientific and Engineering Personnel in which CWSE is housed, for her support and guidance to CWSE during coordination of the symposium.

Howard Georgi, Ph.D., *Co-chair*
Lilian Shiao-Yen Wu, Ph.D., *Co-chair*
Committee on Women in
Science and Engineering

Contents

PLENARY PANEL IV: ADVANCING WOMEN INTO SCIENCE LEADERSHIP

Figures

FIGURES

WHO WILL DO THE SCIENCE OF THE FUTURE?

Marye Anne Fox (Moderator)
Chancellor, North Carolina State University

Overview

Welcome to a very important symposium entitled, "Who Will Do the Science of the Future? A Symposium on Careers of Women in Science."

I am Marye Anne Fox, and I will moderate the discussion today. I do so at the request of the Council of the National Academy of Sciences (NAS) on which I currently serve as a member.

Every year at the annual meeting the women members of the NAS get together to discuss issues facing members of groups under-represented in the Academy's membership. Unfortunately, that meeting is quite small. So, we are very pleased today to welcome to this session a larger group, including both our colleagues in the NAS and many other guests. All of us in the National Academy of Sciences thank you sincerely for being here.

It is striking that if you look at university populations today, compared with the nation's demographic distribution, you will find significant differences between the student body and the general population. In particular, these differences are quite evident by race and ethnic group. If you continue the same exercise to other university groups, moving from students through the faculty and through the administrative leadership you will find that these differences become ever more obvious.

Think, for example, about various academic groupings, first the students, then the faculty, then the tenured faculty, then chaired professors, then the upper administration, and then members of the National Academies of Sciences and Engineering. You find a group distribution that is increasingly white and increasingly male. And, significantly, these distortions have persisted despite more than three decades of people of goodwill working hard at opening access and opportunity to all.

To look at the academic future, one should focus on the graduate student population. Although this group has traditionally been dominated by white males, you will find fewer white males in the current group than was true 20 years ago, since there are increasingly numbers of foreign nationals, as well as more women and members of ethnic and racial groups. Fewer native-born men are pursuing graduate degrees in science and engineering. Hence the question, the title of the seminar, "Who Will Do the Science of the Future?" at a time when the demographic trends in this nation predict native-born white males to be a minority group in the very near future.

In that context, our program incorporates three panels of presentations: one focusing on the next generation, Science for All Students; a second that looks in depth at the issues reflected in one particular field of science, computer science, reflecting an in-depth view of academic and industrial computer scientists; and a third that focuses on strategies and policies to recruit, retain, and promote career advancement for women scientists. Finally, we will have a plenary address on how to ensure women continue to advance into positions of leadership in science.

We will begin with remarks from Dr. Bruce Alberts, the President of the National Academy of Sciences and Chair of the National Research Council, the principal operating arm of the National Academies of Sciences and Engineering. Dr. Alberts is a respected biochemist, recognized for his work in biochemistry and molecular biology. He is noted particularly for his extensive study of protein complexes that allow chromosomes to be replicated as required for a living cell to divide. In addition, he is the principal author of "The Molecular Biology of the Cell," which is considered the leading textbook in its field, and is widely used in colleges and universities here and abroad.

Dr. Alberts has long been committed to the improvement of science education, having dedicated much of his time to educational projects such as City Science, a program seeking to improve science teaching in San Francisco elementary schools. He has served on the Advisory Board of The National Sciences Resource Center, a joint project of the National Academy of Sciences and the Smithsonian Institution, that works with teachers, students, and school systems to improve the teaching of science, as well as on the National Academy of Sciences' Committee on Science Education, Standards and Assessments.

Bruce Alberts, President
National Academy of Sciences

Welcome

I would like to thank the Steering Committee and Marye Anne for organizing this symposium. This is the first time that we have ever had such an event at our annual meeting.

The members of the Steering Committee, in addition to Marye Anne Fox were Margaret Burbidge, Mildred Cohn, Millie Dresselhaus, Maria New, Vera Rubin, and Karen Uhlenbeck. We also need to thank the co-chairs of our Committee on Women in Science and Engineering, Lilian Wu and Howard Georgi. I'm very appreciative of their continued efforts on this important issue.

We all recognize that science is, and must be, an elitist enterprise. It needs our very best minds. Unfortunately, we turn many, probably most, of those potential scientists away from science at an early age. When we do so, we are shortchanging both science and our nation.

To date, science has never really looked like America. It has always been carried out predominantly by white males. But included are immigrants from all over the world participating in science. Therefore, no matter where talent arises, our enterprise recognizes it without regard to the culture or the country of origin of the individual.

Science is a merit-based enterprise. How do we bring more people into this enterprise? It is very important that we do so for many reasons. One often talks about the unfairness of not giving everybody a chance to contribute. But an even bigger issue in this country, as it becomes more and more diverse, is that a science establishment run primarily by white males runs the danger of alienating our nation and our people from science.

In my field of biology, my university, the University of California, San Francisco (UCSF) has been competing with MIT for the very best graduate students in the nation. For at least 10 years now, over half of these graduate students have been women.

In biology, women are doing very well as undergraduates and in graduate school. We need to understand what follows afterward. This is an important issue that could be scientifically studied.

Our symposium today is designed to encourage discussion about the efforts that are being made by some of our very best scientists to bring more diversity to science at all levels, and you will hear about some important ideas.

As you heard, the Academy has a committee that is being informed by this symposium today and will be empowered by it. In the process of working on this issue, we want to make science appear to everyone as what it truly is: a wonderful enterprise, a worldwide enterprise in which anyone with talent, ambition, and interest can participate. If we do that, science will have a much larger role, both in this nation and the world.

Plenary Panel I:

The Next Generation: Science for All Students

Marye Anne Fox (Moderator)
Chancellor, North Carolina State University

SPEAKER INTRODUCTIONS

The first panel of our program will focus on the next generation of scientists, "Science for All Students." We have three panelists participating in this discussion: Drs. Leon Lederman, Richard Tapia, and Marcia Linn.

Dr. Lederman is an internationally renowned high-energy physicist, the Director Emeritus of Fermi National Accelerator Laboratory in Batavia, Illinois. He holds an appointment as the Pritzker Professor of Science at Illinois Institute of Technology in Chicago.

Dr. Lederman served as Chairman of the State of Illinois' Governor's Science Advisory Committee, and he is the founder and resident scholar at the Illinois Mathematics and Science Academy, a three-year residential public high school for the gifted. Dr. Lederman was Director of the Fermi Laboratory from 1979 to 1989, and is a founder and Chairman of the Teachers' Academy for Mathematics and Science. In 1990, he was elected President of the

American Association for the Advancement of Science. He served as a founding member of the High-Energy Physics Advisory Board of the United States Department of Energy and on the International Committee for Future Accelerators, the largest organization of that type in the United States. He is a member of the National Academy of Sciences and has received numerous awards, including the National Medal of Science, the Elliott Cresson Medal of the Franklin Institute, the Wolf Prize in Physics, and the Nobel Prize in Physics.

Dr. Richard Tapia is a strong advocate for minorities and women in the sciences and mathematics, and is a professor in the Department of Computational and Applied Mathematics at Rice University in Houston.

In addition to being the first in his family to attend college, Dr. Tapia is also the first native-born Hispanic American to be inducted into the National Academy of Engineering. Internationally known for his research and work in computational and mathematical science, he was appointed by President William Clinton to the National Science Board in 1996. Recently, Dr. Tapia became the co-editor for all educational outreach programs for the nation's two supercomputer centers in San Diego and the University of Illinois.

Dr. Marcia Linn is a Professor of Development and Cognition and of Education in Mathematics, Science and Technology in the Graduate School of Education at the University of California at Berkeley.

A fellow of the American Association for the Advancement of Sciences, she researches the teaching and learning of science and technology, gender equity and the design of technological learning environments. In 1998, the Council of Scientific Society Presidents selected her for its first award in educational research. From 1995 to 1996, she was a fellow at the Center for Advanced Study in Behavioral Sciences, and in 1994 she received the National Association for Research and Science Teaching Award for Life-Long Distinguished Contributions to Science Education.

The American Educational Research Association bestowed on her the Willystine Goodsell Award in 1991, and the Women Educators Research Award in 1982. Twice she has won the Outstanding Paper Award from the Journal of Research in Science Teaching. She serves on the Board of the American Association for the Advancement of Science, the Graduate Record Examination Board of the Educational Testing Service, and the McDonnell Foundation for Cognitive Studies in Education.

Dr. Leon M. Lederman, *Director Emeritus*
Fermi National Accelerator Laboratory

A PLAN, A STRATEGY FOR K-12

When I was invited to come here I said, "Well, the only thing I could talk about is what I happen to be doing now, and I happen to be very interested in high schools and high school science." I spend a lot of time in high schools. I didn't know how relevant I could make that to your topic but between that time and now I have learned that indeed the kinds of things I am after have a surprising relevance to the issue we have today.

I am going to talk about a plan, a strategy for getting into the K-12 arena in a dramatic way. Now, again, my problem is complicated by the fact that I am a limited observer in this field. I tend to look at the spectrum of opinions on science education in the country, say, ever since the 16-year-old report, *A Nation at Risk*. One can read justifiable opinions on all sides of how well we are doing.

My own feeling is more pessimistic. In spite of the expenditure of many hundreds of millions of dollars invested in science education reform and efforts of many, many smart people, we have very little to show for it.

It is not that we don't have anything to show for it. We certainly have a keen awareness now of the importance of science. Most dramatically, in spite of the obsessive belief in local deployment of education, we have a consensus of national standards in math and science that are being adopted by many states. The National Academies played an important role in this crucial development.

We are interested in a dramatic reform of high school science education, designed to change the way science is taught in 99 percent of U.S. high schools. We also want to breach the wall of resistance to change that seems to surround our educational system, and like any military strategist, once you enter that breach you spread out and begin to make the changes appropriate for the 21st century.

I call it TYNT because most teachers, when you talk to them about reform, will say, "Oh, oh, that is This Year's New Thing." You have to face the fact that schools are bombarded with "This Year's New Things." Of course, *my* year's new thing is going to be different from all other "This Year's New Things."

We call it the "American Renaissance In Science Education," or ARISE, and I like the word "renaissance." It is carefully chosen. Three happenings make things encouraging. One is the new science standards. These standards require a minimum of three years of science in the grade 9-12 program. Four is better, if you want to reach and exceed the standards. Then we have the problem of the international tests like the Third International

Mathematics & Science Study (TIMSS) 1998 and other assessments that tell us that we have a long way to go before we can be satisfied with our educational system. The poor performance of our students cries out for reform.

Finally, the time is appropriate to make serious changes in education, which has become known as "dot edu." The President of the United States says that improving education is the most important thing we can do in the nation and this is clearly an unimpeachable source.

We have about 16,000 school districts in this country, all going in their own different directions. About 50 percent of these schools insist on more than one year of science. Only 20 percent insist on three years of science, but there is a trend now to increasing the science required as states begin to take on the problem of establishing standards. Many, if not most, states are aligning their standards pretty nearly with the national consensus standards written by the Academies and by the American Association for the Advancement of Science.

I think we see a good trend of increasing the science requirement. ARISE proposes to create a coherent three-year curriculum. That is, once you have a three-year science requirement, you may as well make it a core curriculum and let it hang together. We use the word "coherent" and "core curriculum" because we want to show that there is a logical order to the disciplines and strong connecting links.

If you look at the mathematical metaphor, you study addition, and then you study subtraction, and you study lots of things in mathematics, but you never forget addition because you keep using it. It isn't a question of learning addition and then forgetting it because you are doing some other mathematics. It is all built in and is coherent.

In science, there is a natural tendency to move from the concrete to the abstract. We like inquiry methods, connections, applications, and the use of what we have learned as we advance; these are the sort of criteria relevant to a coherent science requirement. A model that satisfies all of these principles is a three-year core science curriculum woven appropriately in with mathematics. You could call it science 1, 2, and 3, but science 1, which would be ninth grade, would be mostly physics, using the algebra that students are just learning in eighth and ninth grade. It implies conversations between the math teacher and the physics teacher. Conceptual physics deals with some of the concrete things in the world around us, such as Michael Jordan's hang time.

Conceptual physics in ninth grade would include forces, motion, energy, gravity, circular motion, electricity, and electrical and magnetic forces. After a year of the standard treatments of physics, using only ninth grade math, stressing concepts, you end up with kids who have a feeling for atoms—the structure and function of atoms. Some elements of quantum theory are needed to understand how atoms differ from one another, some idea of the shells which electrons populate as we proceed from the simplest atom, hydrogen, to the more complicated atoms with many electrons. Presto! You are already beginning to explain that colorful chart which appears in one billion chemistry classrooms around the world, which is called the periodic table of the elements. Now the student, building on his or her year of physics, has a mechanism for understanding not only why the periodic table is the way it is, but also how the chemical properties are read from the table.

Tenth grade would be mostly chemistry. You have already begun chemistry. You continue with a higher level of mathematics (i.e., tenth grade) and little by little you proceed through the standard chemical processes, which continuously exercise the physics as a basis for understanding. The energy viewpoint teaches why some atoms approach one another and bind to form simple molecules. Gas laws and solutions again make use of the properties of atoms. Eventually one gets to molecules, which are large enough so that one or two of them start talking to you, and then the class realizes that they are already in biology. This is the kind of biology that is so exciting these days. It is molecular based, and we are assured that the 21st century will be the century of biology, according to our unimpeachable source.

A century is a long time to make predictions. For certain, the science and technology of the new biology will dominate the beginning. However, today in 99 percent of all high schools, biology, chemistry, and physics is the order in which students study science. Ninth grade biology is descriptive, probably that kind of descriptive biology which should be in middle school, but here it is, full of new vocabulary . . . more new words than in ninth grade French!

Ninth grade biology doesn't make sense and the students know it. The sequence, biology, chemistry, physics is universal not only because it is alphabetical, but also because it was proposed by a very wise committee more than one hundred years ago. The fact that we continue to do it wrong in our schools, in spite of the progress in our science knowledge, is remarkable. In the 1930s, we learned the power of physics to understand basic chemical processes and then certainly in the fifties after the discovery of deoxyribonucleic acid (DNA), it became totally clear that biology must be preceded by both chemistry and physics. The resistance of the system to change, you will have to admit, is awesome.

Implications of a sensible, coherent curriculum in the correct order are very significant. Physics, chemistry, biology, and math teachers have to talk to each other at least four hours a week. It is not an easy thing to implement. You need a lot of conversations so that you can maintain and extend this coherence. Now, if you are meeting with physics, chemistry, biology, and math teachers it is already a pretty big crowd. You may as well invite the history, art, and literature teachers and begin the process of expanding the breach into a more unified approach to all of education in the high schools, a 21st century "renaissance" of learning.

The goal of our physics-first sequence is science as a way of thinking designed to generate comfort with new ideas and with new situations so characteristic of our times.

In a three-year science sequence, one must include lots of pedagogic excursions to real world problems, sometimes contrived and sometimes real, that include interdisciplinary and transdisciplinary approaches. These provide a link to the other disciplines. Teaching science without some appeal to its history, how do we know, how did we go wrong, and so forth, is dry as dust.

This new curriculum is for *all* students. Out of this, for students who might be interested in further science, there would be Advanced Placement courses or fourth-year elective courses. There are many things you can do for all students whether their future is jobs, liberal arts, or science and technology. There is also the hope of trying to do something about the famous two-culture gap, by giving all of our high school graduates of the 21st century a feeling for the essential unity of knowledge, emphasized perhaps by the variety in ways of knowing and thinking. Before one dismisses this as hopeless, one should think through the earning potential of such a graduate.

Now, let me get quickly to the relevance of all of this to this assembly. In advertising this stuff, in getting it in the *New York Times*, *Science* Magazine, NPR's *Science Friday*, and so forth, we became aware that there exists an array of high schools already doing a physics-first sequence.

We now have a listserv of 70 high schools around the nation—some private, some public—that are doing what they call "physics first."

Some of these schools have been doing this for upward of 12 years. The reports we are getting from these schools are so extremely favorable that the physicist in me gets a little suspicious. How could it be so good? We hear that after the new sequence is installed, increases take place in fourth-year science electives, enrollment in AP science courses zooms up, college successes are recorded, and then, here is the funny thing, there is a dramatic effect on women and minority students from poor families who come into high school without a strong positive science and math experience. Many of these schools tell us things like: "AP physics now has 53 percent women." I remember AP physics as having one, two, or no women. What is going on?

One can have theories as to why this happens. Perhaps it is ninth grade physics, which is largely conceptual physics and doesn't really exercise more math than the students are already learning at that point. Perhaps it is a kinder, gentler introduction to science. Maybe ninth grade biology with its huge memorization and no real analytical processes is a turnoff. It seems to me that we must authenticate this.

We now have a couple of graduate students in science education who are going to visit all the schools we can locate and quantify the data exactly: how many students go in, what happened before, and what happened afterwards. Anecdotally, the data we have now are very impressive as to the influence a coherent science sequence has on women and minority students actually staying in science, taking AP courses, taking fourth-year electives, and so on. If the data holds up, then we must try to understand why, and of course we must realize that if 70 or 200 schools are doing it right, we only have 15,697 high schools left to convince.

Richard Tapia, Professor
Computational and Applied Mathematics,
Rice University

MENTORING MINORITY WOMEN IN SCIENCE:
SPECIAL STRUGGLES

What I am going to do is share with you some of my experiences. I will somewhat deviate from the assigned task that I was given and share with you that which I know best. It certainly is an important part of the conference theme.

Representation of minority women Ph.D.s in the hard sciences is a big national failure. By hard sciences I mean the mathematical sciences, physics, and computer science.

Minority women comprise 75 percent of the undergraduate students at minority-serving institutions. These are the Historically Black Colleges and Universities (HBCUs) and the University of Puerto Rico and the Hispanic-serving institutions. Women are significantly well represented in the hard sciences at the undergraduate level in these schools. Minority women, both African American and Hispanic, out-earn their male counterparts in total Ph.D.s.

Minority men are greatly underrepresented in the hard sciences compared to majority men, and our small minority representation in the hard sciences is predominantly male, not female. The conclusion is: minority women are on the move, but not in the hard-sciences Ph.D.s. They are not encouraged and are not retained in the Ph.D. hard-science programs.

The country's dilemma then falls into the following situations: there are basically no minorities in the hard sciences, and we are headed for serious problems in terms of representation; the minority men are becoming an endangered species in post-secondary education. They don't go into undergraduate and particularly graduate school, and minority women do not enter or are not retained through the Ph.D. level in the hard sciences.

We can conjecture on possible blame— culture, society, and faculty culture. Faculty culture is something that I would like to address. I may say some things that people don't follow well or disagree with. So, let me give you the basis on which I developed these ideas.

In my career, at Rice, I have had 36 Ph.D. students. Fifteen of them have been women. My first student was a woman. She wrote an outstanding dissertation. Recently, Herb Keller at CalTech called me and said, "Richard, I was going to do a research project with a student, and I found that your student Mary Ann McCarthy had already done it, an excellent dissertation."

Last year I had two minority Ph.D. students, two women. This year I had three minority Ph.D. students in the mathematical sciences, one African American, two Mexican Americans, all women. At times, our department puts out half the productivity of minority women math Ph.D.s in the United States. My graduate class in optimization consists of five women, no men. They are all my students. Three are minorities.

Certainly, a part of the success comes from my commitment, strong critical mass in our department, strong structured mentoring, and a support system. I would like to address the mentoring and the support system.

Our support system has received a lot of recognition, and it is the basis for the NSF Minority Graduate Education Award that we just received. We were the only school west of the Mississippi that received such an award.

My premise is the following: there exist significant differences between men, women, and minorities. The problems of women and minorities are different. Minority women share both. Women and minorities should not be lumped into the same category for purposes of correcting issues.

African Americans are different from Hispanics and Native Americans, especially foreign versus domestic. Mainland Puerto Ricans, affectionately called New Yoricans, share similarities with African Americans. Mexican Americans, somewhat affectionately called Chicanos, are similar to Native Americans, with very strong ties. Strangers are often confused by me. Am I Native American or am I Mexican American?

In the Houston Independent School District, where I am very involved, success or failure in a K-12 class can be a function of understanding the various Hispanic/Latino populations and the great variants among them.

Successful mentoring is facilitated by understanding these differences. You under- stand the individual better, and this builds trust and respect. You become a credible individual.

Certainly, I find that women talk about their problems a lot easier than men. They also feel that they have the need to talk about this issue. Minorities and women tend to lean toward scientific areas that directly impact our lives or society; i.e., most of the women and minorities that I work with are in some aspect of computational biology, computational medicine, and so forth.

Minorities in majority schools have a strong need to be involved in some form of outreach so that they don't feel that they have turned their backs to their people. A part of my mentoring program involves minorities and women in outreach, but not to the extent that it endangers their careers.

Majority schools produce leaders. We need minority leaders. This is the point of the Bowen and Bok book, *The Shape of the River.* We need minority leaders. Majority schools produce majority leaders.

This point often seems to be missed. My argument is that underrepresentation endangers first the health of the nation, but not the health of the profession. The profession is going to live. Two disjoint cycles, minority and majority, are not healthy for the nation or the profession.

Special challenges that I share with you are these: women and minorities are extremely risk averse. I don't feel that they are born that way. I think it is something that we learn, but women and minorities are extremely risk averse, afraid of failure, and don't want it discovered that maybe they don't know something.

Minority women suffer from being members of both groups. It is often very difficult for minority women to make bold conjectures. Let

me share with you a letter from a colleague of mine who is directing two minority women that I mentor, and he says to me, "Richard, I have been thinking a lot about A and B, both minority women and what this all means. It struck me that I see them both failing in the same way. They are incredibly risk averse. They just will not take a chance. They won't even attempt work that they are not sure about. They won't speak up in seminar. They won't even bug me when they don't understand something for fear of my reaction; no risk, no learning. What in this world makes them so unwilling to risk failure and therefore sure of experiencing it? It must be a helluva place for both of them, extremely dangerous. Is there anything we can do to fix this? I don't know. It is not role models that they are missing."

If we don't change this, we are going to find women and minorities who will be good scientists, good scientist assistants, good technicians, but certainly they will not take a leadership role in science.

When I say this about minorities, it is not exclusive to minorities. Everybody shares these things. I just think the problem is magnified within the minority community.

Consider the fulfillment of womanhood, motherhood, and extended family. Traditional culture dictates a dream with expectation of dating, marrying, raising children near their grandparents and family, and then grandchildren. Science culture sells an opportunity for them to either have no husband or a late marriage, no children or few and late, live away from the extended family, much stress, little relaxation. It is a very hard sell that women have to deal with. The family doesn't promote the sell. The family says, "Look, you are 30 years old. You are not married, and you are still going to school."

Consider another issue; minority women are attracted to minority men, but these men will not let them be the women that they want to be in terms of reaching out. When I am adviser to the minority communities at Rice, I deal with this issue all the time. When at Stanford, I dealt with that issue all the time. In the community they also have to deal with machismo, which is a part of the culture.

Also, no doubt about it, minority women identify with both groups, the minority group and the women. However, there is a conflict. There is a split. I have never had a minority woman claim a stronger identification to the women's movement than the minority movement. The implication is that there is more unmerited discriminatory behavior and more difficult problems there. I asked my wife yesterday about this. My wife is New Yorican. She said, "That is an interesting question, Richard," and then she said, "Of course, the minority thing."

It is interesting that when we have meetings like a recent Sloan Conference, that was a controversial issue. In fact, every minority woman said, "Identification to minority issues." Every majority woman said, "It shouldn't be

that way." It is hard for them to accept this issue.

The faculty traditional hiring process is not fair to women and is extremely unfair to minorities. They are seen as not being sufficiently precocious, no theorems before the age of 25, and graduating with a Ph.D. at the age of 30.

I bring you a message from my women students. I told them that I was going to address this distinguished group. My women students got together and said, "Here are the kinds of things we would like for you to share with them: Mentoring is not something that you do from two to three on Monday, Wednesday, and Friday. It is something that you do at all times and in particular when the need arises and in the problem areas. We are not aware of the fact that we are being mentored or that we need mentoring. It is a part of our everyday experience and our professional training. Some faculty are terrible at mentoring. Not all faculty should mentor."

I conclude with this: role models are not necessarily successful women or women of color. For the women that I work with, Mary Wheeler has played a strong role and has been a role model. Men can be very effective mentors for women. What is important in good mentoring is sensitivity to the special struggles that women and especially minority women face.

Marcia C. Linn, Professor
Development and Cognition,
University of California, Berkeley

CONTROVERSY, THE INTERNET,
AND DEFORMED FROGS:
MAKING SCIENCE ACCESSIBLE

This material is based upon research supported by the National Science Foundation under grants EEC-9053807, MDR-9155744, RED-9453861, and DGE-9554564. Any opinions, findings, and conclusions or recommendations expressed in this publication are those of the authors and do not necessarily reflect the views of the National Science Foundation. Special thanks to all the members of the *Deformed Frogs!* partnership, including the classroom teachers, the discipline specialists, the technology experts, and the students who have and will participate in the project.

I challenge all concerned about science education to remedy the serious declines in science interest, the disparities in male and female persistence in science, and the public resistance to scientific understanding by forming partnerships to bring to life the excitement and controversy in scientific research. Science controversies can offer students a window on science in the making and showcase the diverse voices contributing to scientific discourse. Communicating a sense of the excitement that sustains and nurtures our quest for scientific understanding can infect students with a quest for lifelong science learning. When students see that scientists regularly revisit their ideas and rethink their views, students are empowered to do the same.

Giving students the opportunity to connect to a contemporary scientific controversy can establish valuable lifelong science learning patterns. Unlike typical science instruction, curriculum materials that feature current scientific controversies are more easily connected to the problems and concerns that students will face in their lives. They can prepare students to make decisions on other controversial science topics such as alternative medical treatments, environmental stewardship, nutrition, or smoking. In making decisions all during their lives, students will typically encounter controversial and conflicting material from diverse sources including scientific journals, news reports, testimonials, and the Internet. Science courses that incorporate this information into the curriculum can equip students to think critically and productively about new science topics.

This challenge of making sense of diverse findings motivates scientists, yet rarely occurs for science learners. Today, controversy in science is erased from the published record, obliterated from the science textbook, yet privileged in the popular press! Articles in scientific journals tend to focus on the results, often telling a rather uncontroversial story of hypothesis, resolution, and consensus (Latour,

1998; Lemke, 1990). Textbooks devote less than 1 percent of the material to controversy; the most common Internet science assignment is to read a few Web pages. It is no wonder that many students report that everything in the science textbook is currently true, with the possible exception of some of the true-false questions. Unless we design the curriculum carefully, they may also conclude that Internet materials are generally accurate. Rather than seeing science as a dynamic enterprise where scientists make sense of complex topics, students see science primarily as a collection of facts. When asked whether they should memorize science information or understand it, many students respond that memorization works the best (Linn & Hsi, 1999). Students distinguish classroom science textbook material from popular press accounts of scientific controversies, and often conclude that scientists are simply perverse and disagree with each other in the popular media because they do not want to change their minds. As a result, students may isolate the material learned in school and assume that it lacks relevance to science information they will encounter in their lives.

For example, when we ask middle school students whether science is relevant to their lives, many say, "No, there is nothing that I have learned in science that I can use in my life." Others, like a student I will call Terry, give a superficial answer saying, "Yes, because there is science all around you. Almost everything has something to do with science." When the interviewer asks, "Is it relevant outside of school?" Terry responds, "Yes, it is just not the same as what we do in school. It is just that is in school, and that is at home. So, the stuff is different, you know?" When the interviewer persists, asking, "How is it different?" Terry replies, "Well, I mean at home that would be like if you really found something. This [science class] is like all set up, you know?" Terry separates school science from the out-of-school process of scientific inquiry. Consistent with Terry's comments, students have been heard to remark, "Objects in motion remain in motion in science class, but come to rest at home."

Introducing the Deformed Frog Controversy

To remedy the lack of connection between school science and lifelong learning, we engaged students in exploring a contemporary controversy about frog deformities. We formed a partnership at Berkeley with graduate students from David Wake's laboratory, technology experts, assessment experts, pedagogical researchers, classroom teachers from a local

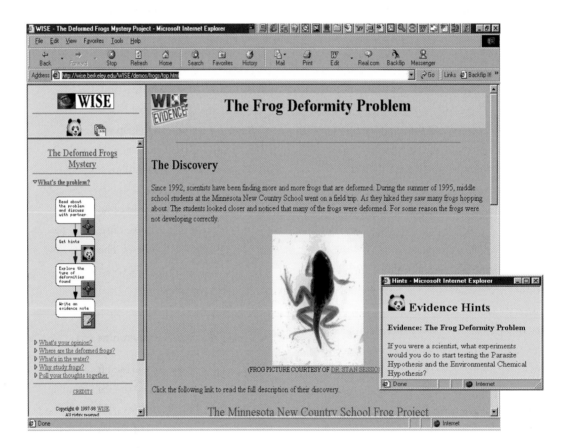

FIGURE 1 The WISE environment introduces the frog deformity problem with reports from a middle school in Minnesota and asks students to predict how scientists might respond.

middle school, and middle school students (see http://wise.berkeley.edu).

The deformed frogs controversy motivates diverse students for many reasons. There is the "yuck, gross" factor. In addition, the topic was publicized in 1995 by a group of school children who discovered deformed frogs while on a fieldtrip to a pond in Minnesota (Figure 1). Students have returned to local ponds and documented increasing deformities. In some ponds, up to 80 percent of the frogs are deformed and some communities are distributing bottled water. Finally, the controversy connects to student concerns about environmental stewardship.

A contemporary controversy like deformed frogs can bring diverse voices of scientists to light in the classroom. Scientists in laboratories researching the controversy have created informative, accessible Internet materials (e.g., Lab for *Studies of Regeneration* and *Deformed Frogs* http://darwin.bio.uci.edu/~mrjc/; *Deformed Amphibian Research* at http:// www.hartwick.edu/biology/def_frogs/).

We are investigating effective ways to help students use Internet materials to construct their own arguments and prepare for a classroom debate (see Linn et al., 1999). To help students understand this controversy, our partnership organized the Internet material around two main hypotheses. The parasite hypothesis says that increases in a parasite called a trematode explain the increase in frog deformities. Scientists can show that trematodes get into frog limb buds during metamorphosis and either block limb growth or enable multiple limbs to grow. The environmental chemical hypothesis says that increases in chemicals used

to spray adjacent fields get into the pond water and cause the increase in deformities. In particular, methoprene, a chemical found in some pesticides, is closely related to retinoids, a growth hormone that has been shown to cause deformities in many organisms including frogs and humans.

To investigate the controversy, students examine a variety of evidence from several research laboratories, discuss their ideas with peers, search for additional information, form arguments, and participate in a debate. Students often bring in news articles about frog deformities both during the unit and after they have completed the unit. As a result, students can connect their science learning to out-of-school experiences and also revisit their ideas after completing classroom instruction.

The partnership constantly seeks additional evidence from research to help students revise their ideas and reconsider their views. For example, the partnership identified research on Lefty (Figure 2) as a pivotal case because the legs growing out of its stomach, rather than at the limb buds, raises doubts about the parasite hypothesis. The partnership seeks compelling results like these to spur student thinking.

Designing the Learning Environment

The partnership also benefited from a 15-year long research project called the *Computer as Learning Partner* (http://www.clp.berkeley.edu) that informed the design of the Web-based Integrated Science Environment used to deliver curriculum (WISE, http://wise.berkeley.edu). The cognitive and social research findings from

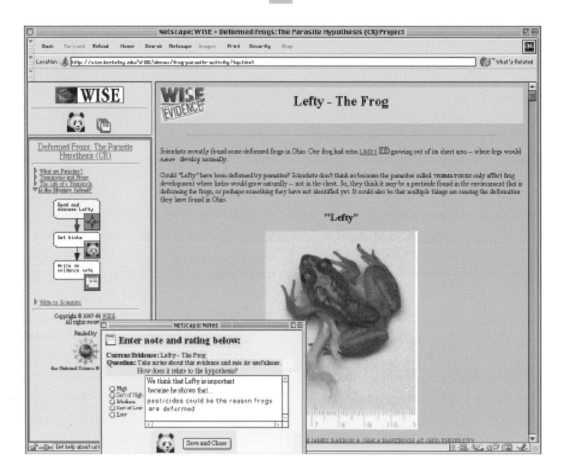

FIGURE 2 Students critique a research report on Lefty the Frog using their knowledge of the parasite hypothesis.

this research enabled the *Deformed Frogs!* partnership to get a head start on curriculum design. For example, as shown in Figure 2, the environment captures the inquiry process graphically on the left side of the screen. This inquiry map appears in every activity that students do using WISE giving students a consistent representation of the inquiry process. The WISE learning environment enabled the partnership to create controversy materials that draw on Internet materials and take advantage of classroom research.

The WISE inquiry map guides students to critique Web material, seek hints, respond to prompts by reflecting on ideas, and to question the source and validity of each Web site. Using WISE, students review evidence, take notes, get hints, discuss with peers, organize their ideas, and plan their debate presentation. Students can also participate in an on-line, asynchronous

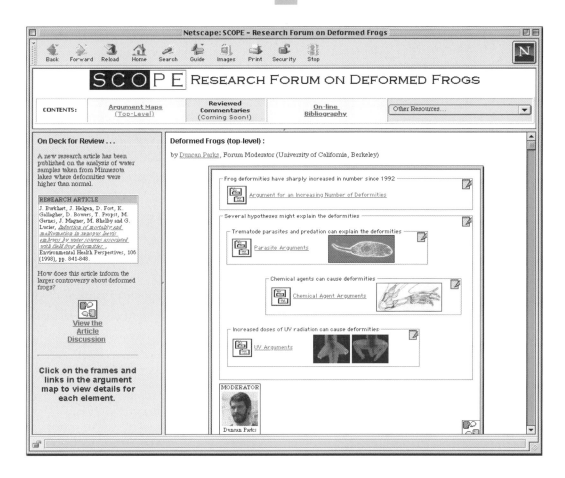

FIGURE 3 Duncan Parks, a member of the *Deformed Frogs!* partnership, created this visual representation of an argument using the same Internet evidence available to students.

discussion of specific questions relevant to the controversy such as: "How do laboratory experiments compare to studies of frogs found in the wild?" The learning environment structures the activities, helps students explore the controversy, encourages them to follow a consistent inquiry process, and frees the teachers to focus primarily on helping students develop their arguments.

To help students recognize that scientists can construe evidence differently in a contemporary controversy, we are gathering diverse perspectives on controversial topics. In a new project called Science Controversies On-line: Partnerships in Education (SCOPE) partnership, scientists represent their arguments and identify open questions using a visual representation as shown in Figure 3. Students can compare their representations to those of several scientists (see http://scope.educ.washington.edu).

Designing the Debate

Engaging students in debate is a novel activity for science class. The partnership spent a considerable amount of time honing and refining the debate activity to make it equitable and effective. Often, class discussions engage only a few students and privilege male views. To ensure that students connect all their ideas— not just classroom information—we developed a comprehensive classroom debate activity. Students had the opportunity to learn from each other and to respect diverse views.

To make the debate accessible, the partnership sought ways to frame the two hypotheses about frog deformities: parasites and environmental chemicals. The scientist members of the partnership initially framed the environmental chemical hypothesis in terms of the chemical similarity between methoprene and retinoids. The teachers pointed out that students in seventh and eighth grade had not studied chemistry, and therefore would not be able to make good sense of these chemical representations. The scientists and teachers looked for a way to analyze the environmental chemical hypothesis that captured the main issues in the controversy without frustrating students with details that were unfamiliar to them. The goal was to maintain the controversial character of this debate and to make sure that it was meaningful to the students. (See Linn & Muilenberg, 1995, for additional discussion of the level of analysis issue.) Rather than chemical representations, the partnership used a descriptive representation describing the character of the similarities. The teachers helped students to connect chemical similarities to other cases of mistaken identity.

The partnership selected cleared and stained frogs as a representation of the nature of the deformities that students could interpret. Students could analyze the shape and form of the deformities by looking at these skeletons. Students could compare cleared and stained frogs that had been exposed to different conditions. For example, students could contrast the appearance of limb deformities when frogs were raised under carefully controlled conditions in the laboratory and when frogs matured under more complex conditions in the wild.

The second main hypothesis, the parasite hypothesis, was easy to frame once the focus on cleared and stained frogs was made. For example, results from the "bead experiment" where researchers blocked limb growth using resin beads were easily compared to results from blockage because of parasites. The teachers worked with scientists to transform research descriptions into prose likely to communicate to students. For example, the term, "Mirror image limb duplications" needed to be unpacked and illustrated in order for students to understand it. We also added a glossary and supports for language learners. Three design decisions show how the partnership engaged students in scientifically responsible communication about a complex topic.

The teachers, scientists, and pedagogical researchers worked together to take Internet Web pages designed by the scientists and add pages that clarified material that students found complex and confusing. After several iterations between teachers and scientists, evidence that was acceptable to both groups and all members of the partnership emerged. The partnership sought to depict this controversy in language and representations that students could understand, without losing the essential excitement and disagreement that existed in the field. The classroom results, discussed below, suggest that the partnership succeeded.

Conducting a Debate in Science Class

The teachers were initially skeptical about introducing debate in science class. One said, "I've never seen a debate in science class." Another remarked, "Students will disrupt, not pay attention." Members of the partnership described successful middle school debates and invited a teacher, experienced in using debate, to meet with the *Deformed Frogs!* partnership and discuss using debate in science class. The partnership observed this teacher use a debate. Teachers asked questions like, "How did students learn to ask such good questions?" or "How can I model good debate behavior?" The teachers agreed to use several practices established by the experienced teacher, including requiring each student to write questions for each presenter and asking all groups to come prepared to debate both sides of the topic. This discussion focused on pedagogical content knowledge (Shulman, 1986). The teachers discussed how to connect science subject matter knowledge and classroom practice knowledge to design a debate that allowed students to link and connect their ideas, to develop a more cohesive and robust understanding of science, and to respect each other.

One of the participating teachers volunteered to try the debate activity. The other teachers were able to observe or watch videos of the teacher enacting the debate. The teachers found that having students write questions down for each presenter meant that that student had the opportunity to think about questions that other presentations raised. In this way, the class as a whole had an opportunity to critique each others' presentations and to learn from every class member.

Each teacher then tried the debate. By repeating the debate in different classrooms, the teachers jointly refined their pedagogical content knowledge about debates concerning *Deformed Frogs!* They defined and identified pivotal cases that helped students shape their arguments. They developed excellent questions to model the questioning process for students. For example, they came up with thought experiments such as, "What would happen if you put adult frogs in water with lots of trematodes?" They also exploited pivotal cases like Lefty the Frog. The debate motivated many students to wonder whether there might be two or more factors at work in frog deformities. Students completed the debate activity and the *Deformed Frogs!* project with an understanding of these two hypotheses and a curiosity about the future.

Classroom Results

Deformed Frogs! activity was carried out with diverse middle school students. Half the students qualify for free or reduced-price lunches and 1 in 4 students speaks English at home. The teachers agreed that *Deformed Frogs!* was successful. One classroom teacher remarked, "Debate helped my students understand that scientists can resolve disputes with evidence."

The quality of students' written questions impressed the teachers.

In the debates, most students were able to make sense of the evidence they encountered on the Internet and to use complex arguments. For example, one sixth grade girl made the following comments: "After the tadpoles grew up, the frogs in fresh methoprene didn't have any deformities in their eyes. But frogs in methoprene that had been in the sun for a while had deformities in the eyes or missing eyes. It proves that sun might play a big role in deforming a frog, but only if it reacts with methoprene." Note that this student not only used complex vocabulary like methoprene and deformities, but also was able to accurately describe the potential interaction between multiple factors, a form of reasoning that rarely occurs in typical science classes.

This example also illustrates that when students are involved in the sustained reasoning and complex argumentation necessary to carry out a debate about this kind of controversy, they learn the vocabulary in the service of science rather than the other way around. Too often students memorize vocabulary only to isolate and forget it. In this case, students have incorporated vocabulary that they can use productively in the future.

The proportion of students turning in assignments was another indication that the controversy activity made science accessible. The teacher of the regular seventh grade science classes reported that her students typically turned in about 67 percent of class assignments. In contrast, 98 percent of her students turned in their *Deformed Frogs!* assignments. She argued that students were more likely to turn in these assignments because they were highly motivated to understand the material.

Teachers also reported that the *Deformed Frogs!* activity gave them another way to evaluate students' ability to learn science. Some of the stars in the debate had never previously engaged in science. The teachers took this as evidence that current instruction was simply not reaching a proportion of students who could be successful. Debate observers, including the school principal, expressed amazement at the contributions of some students who had primarily been viewed as discipline problems in the past. One student, who spent most of science class prior to *Deformed Frogs!* with her head down on her desk, first participated in science during the *Deformed Frogs!* activity. She reported that she participated because the teacher and students cared about her opinion— no one had ever cared about her ideas before. She was a star in the debate presenting a coherent and articulate account of her perspective on the controversy and answering questions effectively. On the class post-test, she persisted for a few pages, complained that written tests are boring, and put her head down.

The *Deformed Frogs!* partnership concurrently designed the pre-tests, post-tests, inquiry activities, and curriculum materials to ensure that instruction and assessment were aligned. One assessment question required students to look at a new deformed frog and explain what they think caused the deformity. Prior to instruction, students gave very general explanations for the possible causes of frog deformities. Students said things like "something in the water" or "something it ate" or "radioactivity." On the post-test, over two-thirds of the students were able to use the mechanism for the parasite hypothesis that they learned from the Internet evidence. One good example of an answer is "Trematodes goes into the limb buds of the tadpole. When tadpole goes through metamorphosis, it deforms frog limbs. It could split a leg into two or stop it from growing." This answer reveals the student to be a language learner. It also captures a complex argument learned from reviewing and integrating the web resources.

Only about one-third of the students could give the fully instructed mechanism concerning the environmental chemical hypothesis on the post-test. We attribute this difference in success to the greater complexity of the environmental chemical hypothesis. In reviewing and revising instruction, we will improve the materials and activities relevant to this hypothesis. On all the assessment measures we found that males and females were equally successful.

Conclusions

Deformed Frogs! enabled diverse students to gain a robust and cohesive understanding of a complex scientific research program. Students could debate using evidence from scientific research. They remained open to future research findings and recognized that the controversy was not yet resolved. They made good connections between their scientific activities in class and science in the wild. They brought news articles into class and reported discussing their science activities with family, friends, and parents. They continued to bring in new articles on the topic all during the school year.

We cannot yet know whether this controversy has set more students on a path toward lifelong learning but we do know that more students participated in science, more students gained scientific understanding, and students became more aware of the excitement that motivates scientists to pursue careers in science. We also observed no differences, in participation or success, for males and females. In related classroom research, we have found that instruction based on this framework does lead to more persistence and interest in science for students from all backgrounds (Linn & Hsi, 1999).

This research project conducted in partnership with teachers, educators, scientists, and technologists demonstrates the challenges associated with designing effective instruction. *Deformed Frogs!* succeeds because the partnership designed the instruction and continues to refine the materials based on classroom research. Too often science instruction is decreed by framework committees or textbook writers rather than designed for the student audience. Students cannot succeed when the instruction is isolated from their ideas or when the assessments lack connection to the curriculum.

The pedagogical framework to promote the linked and coherent understanding students displayed features four main ideas. First, the framework calls for *making science accessible* by crafting an effective representation of a complex controversy, such that students can participate and explore compelling, contemporary scientific ideas. Selecting a level of analysis for environmental chemistry hypotheses was guided by this framework idea. Current controversies make science accessible by enabling students to connect school and personally relevant science ideas, and by illuminating reports in the popular press. Students are concerned about environmental stewardship and connect *Deformed Frogs!* to their views.

Second, the framework calls for *making thinking visible.* Allowing teachers and students to hear diverse voices of scientists is one way to make thinking visible. When scientists model the process of scientific dispute resolution, students observe science in the making and can identify with one scientist or another. The deformed frogs controversy also makes students' ideas visible by offering representations of arguments like the one in Figure 3. Our future work will enable students to compare the argument maps that they create to argument maps created by scientists (http://scope.educ.washington.edu/index.html).

Third, the framework calls for providing diverse opportunities for students to *listen and learn from each other.* Students specialize as they research a controversy and share their experience with others. For example, some students became expert in understanding the staining process and explained how it worked to other students. Most important, students learned from each other during the debate activity by articulating their ideas, asking questions in class, and responding to questions.

Fourth, the framework calls for *promoting lifelong learning.* Enabling students to make connections between what they learn in science class, what they read in the newspaper, hear about on television, or believe about the environment contributes to lifelong learning. By prompting students to reflect on their ideas and to write explanations, we encourage students to reconsider and revisit ideas on their own. In addition, students learned to critique Internet evidence, a skill that they will need in the future. Students asked questions about the origin and authorship of Internet materials. Students became aware that researchers preferred certain methodologies. They noted that some scientists primarily base their assertions on observations of frogs in the wild while other groups preferred to perform laboratory experiments. Students learned to distinguish the potential information value of materials from these different methodological approaches. Students also gained an awareness of the criteria used in different laboratories to evaluate research findings. These ideas can help students as they continue to explore science.

In conclusion, I encourage scientists everywhere to bring contemporary controversies to life to increase the number of students who persist in science. By forming partnerships, including experts in the science disciplines, classroom teaching, pedagogy, and technology, we can create a repertoire of compelling controversies that communicate to students. The WISE learning environment can help by allowing designers to capitalize on current pedagogical research on equitable instruction. Enabling more and more students to make sense of contemporary controversies can also raise public awareness of current science policy issues.

Bibliography

Hellman, H. (1998). Great Feuds in Science. New York: John Wiley & Sons.

Latour, B. (1998). From the World of Science to the World of Research. *Science*, 280 (April 10).

Lemke, J. L. (1990). Talking science: language, learning, and values, (Language and educational processes). Norwood, NJ: Ablex Pub. Corp.

Linn, M. C. & Hsi, S. (1999). Computers, Teachers, Peers: Science Learning Partners. Hillsdale, NJ: Lawrence Erlbaum Associates.

Linn, M. C. & Muilenburg, L. (1995). How can less be more? (Technical Report). Berkeley, CA: University of California at Berkeley, Computer as Learning Partner.

Linn, M. C., Shear, L., Bell, P., & Slotta, J. D. (1999). Organizing principles for science education partnerships: Case studies of students' learning about "rats in space" and "deformed frogs." Educational Technology Research and Development, 47(2), 61-85.

Shulman, L. S. (1986). Those who understand: Knowledge growth in teaching. *Educational Researcher*, 15(2), 4-14.

Plenary Panel II:

An In-Depth View of Computer Science

Marye Anne Fox (Moderator)
Chancellor, North Carolina State University

SPEAKER INTRODUCTIONS

The next panel will focus on computer science and in particular on women and information technology from both an academic and industrial perspective.

Dr. William Wulf is the President of the National Academy of Engineering and Vice Chair of the National Research Council. He is on leave from the University of Virginia, Charlottesville where he is the AT&T Professor of Engineering and Applied Sciences. Among his activities at the university were a complete revision of the undergraduate computer science curriculum, research on computer architecture and computer security, and an effort to assist humanities scholars to exploit information technology.

Dr. Wulf's distinguished professional career has found him serving as Assistant Director for the National Science Foundation, as Chair and Chief Executive Officer of Tartan Laboratories, Inc. in Pittsburgh, and as professor of computer science at Carnegie-Mellon University. He is the author of more than 80 papers and technical reports, has written three books, and holds a patent.

Dr. Lilian Wu is Consultant to Corporate Technical Strategy Development at IBM and a member of the President's Committee of Advisers on Science and Technology. Dr. Wu received her Ph.D. in applied mathematics from Cornell University and her bachelor's degree from the University of Maryland at College Park. Her major research interests are in mathematical modeling and risk analysis in business, particularly in the electric power industry, in women in science and engineering, and in energy and ecosystems.

She serves as the Director of the International Institute of Forecasters and is on the Advisory Boards of the National Institute for Science Education and the Douglas Project for Women in Math, Science and Engineering at Rutgers University.

William A. Wulf, President

National Academy of Engineering

THE DECLINING PERCENTAGE OF WOMEN IN COMPUTER SCIENCE: AN ACADEMIC VIEW

An alternative title for this paper might have been "An Exercise in Self-Flagellation." It is not a happy story I am about to tell you. It is not happy because the ending isn't very happy, and it is not happy because we don't have any explanation for it.

I will present some data on the numbers of degrees in computer science (CS), and then I will present findings from one particular study.

The total number of baccalaureate degrees in computer science awarded peaked in the mid-1980s at about 40,000 (Figure 4). Almost coincident with that, preceding it by a couple of years, the percentage of undergraduate women in computer science peaked at 38 percent of total computer science degrees.

Unfortunately, nobody knows why either of these phenomena occurred. We don't know the reason for the increase to the large number of baccalaureate degrees, accompanied by the increase in percentage of women, in the years leading to the 1980s. Nor do we know the

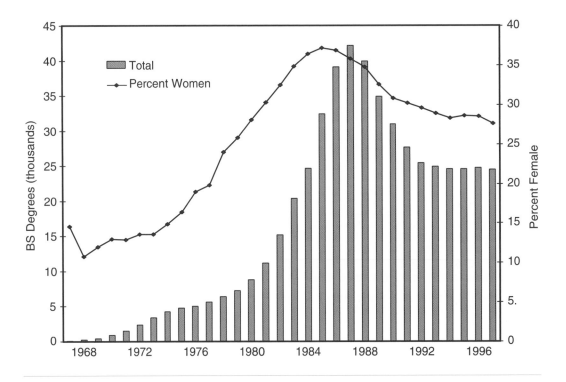

FIGURE 4 Women in computer science.

reasons for the subsequent declines in both the total number of baccalaureate degrees and in the percentage of women.

There are many anecdotal explanations. One thing to understand is that at the time, the field was overwhelmed with undergraduate students. In a visit to the University of Maryland during this period, the computer science department had between 20 or 25 faculty members and 1,500 undergraduates. They were just inundated with students.

When the numbers started to decline, nobody thought to ask *why*. There was just a sense of profound relief.

In particular, no one noticed that the number of women was declining. We were all very proud of the fact that we were approaching 40 percent women undergraduates, and I think we thought that was the natural order of things. So, as things started to drop, surely they were going to go back up again. It didn't happen, and nobody studied why.

Unfortunately, data from the last few years just isn't available yet. In particular, data on incoming students as opposed to graduating ones would be interesting, because the anecdotal evidence is that we are once again experiencing an explosion of undergraduates.

At my own university, the University of Virginia, the number of undergraduates in computer science has roughly quadrupled in the last six or seven years. The same phenomenon is occurring at other colleges and universities. I don't have even anecdotal data on what is happening to the percentage of women, although I am going to tell you about a study that is not encouraging.

Some of the anecdotal reasons given for both the increase and the decline in total number of baccalaureate students note that this is more or less coincident with the release of the personal computer. This explanation posits that the hype associated with IBM's release of the personal computer in 1980, or the availability of machines to a larger number of people, piqued interest. If this is the case, then the current increase in interest may be due to the Internet.

Another explanation is that students thought that if they wanted to have anything to do with computing, they had to be a computer science major. According to this theory, they really were more interested in applying computers to physics or business, but they thought they had to be a computer scientist to do that. The corresponding explanation for the decline is that they realized that it is not true.

Some of my colleagues would like to promulgate the idea that the decline is because students figured out computer science was *hard*, and that it wasn't an easy major.

The data on Ph.D. students is somewhat different. The total number of Ph.D.s graduated per year has climbed to about 1,000 (Figure 5). As with the baccalaureate degrees, cause and

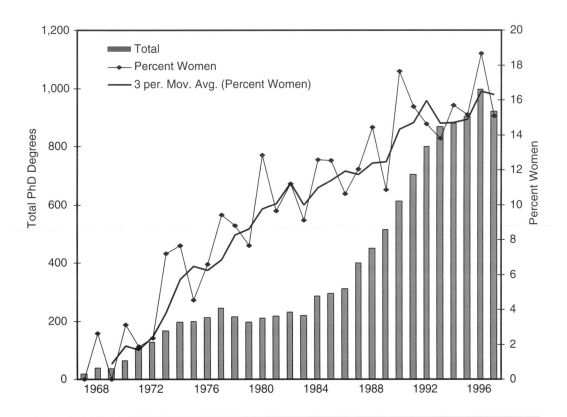

FIGURE 5 Computer science Ph.D.s.

effect are not known, but a report issued about 15 years ago stated that 1,000 computer science Ph.D. students per year was about the right number, and something in the system seems to have converged on that number.

The percentage of women continues to climb a little—a very little. We are seeing an effect here of the law of small numbers. We have lots of fluctuations, and it may actually be flat.

Interestingly, the number of women taking CS courses in high school is almost identical to the number of young men taking CS courses in high school (Figure 6). Broken down further into Advanced Physics (AP) or various kinds of advanced CS courses, again, the numbers are

nearly equal. Yet there is this continuing drop from high school to baccalaureate, to master's, to Ph.D., and to faculty. The numbers for associate and full professors may be related more to the population of women that were available in the cohort. Although it's difficult to discern, we should be concerned that those small numbers may be the result of discrimination in promotion and tenure decisions.

Another issue is the distribution of women in baccalaureate programs in computer science. Currently, the percentage of women receiving baccalaureate degrees in computer science is about 28 percent. That percentage is not uniformly distributed among departments.

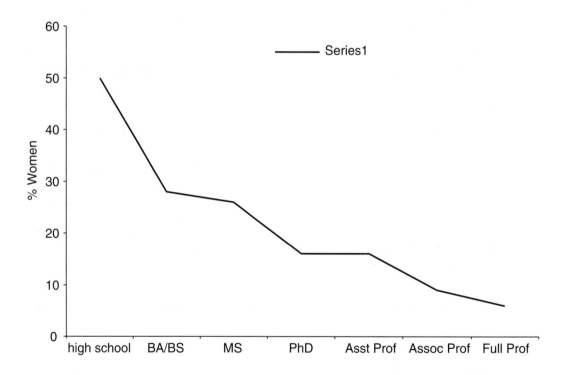

FIGURE 6 The pipeline.

An interesting phenomenon about the discipline is that some CS departments are in engineering schools, some are in colleges of arts and sciences, and some are even their own college.

Of the CS departments that are in engineering schools, some are separate departments and some are combined with electrical engineering. For the years 1991-1993, there is a substantial difference between the number of degrees awarded to women from departments that are in engineering schools (23 percent) and the percentage awarded from departments in colleges of arts and sciences (over 28 percent; Camp, 1998). There is no definitive explanation for this finding.

Now, I will discuss the findings of one particular study. Because at least anecdotally the number of bachelor's degrees is again on the rise, this time perhaps we will collect some data to understand what is actually occurring. The study in question, at Carnegie-Mellon University, attempts to do that (Fisher, Margolis, & Miller, 1997).

The researchers are not looking at the number of women who enter computer science, but rather at the number who entered, and then for one reason or another transferred out. Since the researchers don't know who didn't apply, they are using the transfer-out rate as a surrogate for why students didn't enroll in the first place. The answers they come up with are a little bit different than the usual explanations. One of the things that they can verify is that the nature of the interest of women in computing is quite different from that of men.

Men seem to be interested in computers *per se*. They are fascinated by the device, the programming, and by the mathematics involved.

Women seem to be much more interested in the application of computers to other things. Their real interest is in some other area.

Second, there is the issue of confidence. Although the authors don't have data on this yet, they are studying this issue and may be able to document that there is a real crisis of confidence that happens with women in the first 2 years of their undergraduate programs. In some sense, that is a positive statement, because this is something we can do something about!

Third is this notion that the undergraduates have that you must do all of your work between midnight and 5 a.m., and live on Twinkies and Coke. That doesn't seem to be particularly attractive to women.

Why do men and women get interested in computing? There is a marked gender difference in the number who have been programming since they were very young and expressed an interest in computing *per se* (Figure 7). These data are reversed when they express an interest in using computers to do something else.

Men really seem to enjoy computing *per se* (Figure 8). Women, on the other hand, see this as a much more safe and secure way to gain employment. Women have also been much more influenced by other people, fathers, very often. The notion that computing can be used to do other things tends to be more important to women.

The most troubling and bizarre issue in all of this is the issue of women's lack of confidence in their abilities. The objective measures are that women do just as well as men. There is no difference in grade point average and no

	M	F
• Programming since they were young	38%	10%
• Expressed enthusiasm for computing	73%	25%
• Interest in CS expressed in other areas (e.g., teaching)	9%	40%

Source: Fisher, Margolis & Miller, 1997

FIGURE 7 Interest in computing.

discernible difference in performance. Yet, when interviewed, the women consistently believed that they were not doing as well.

Computer science is unique in that interest in the discipline has varied markedly in a short period of time, and that the driving factor for interest appears to be different for men and women. We need to gather data to allow us to understand the reasons underlying both the fluctuations in interest and the different motivating factors that attract students to computer science. With such an understanding,

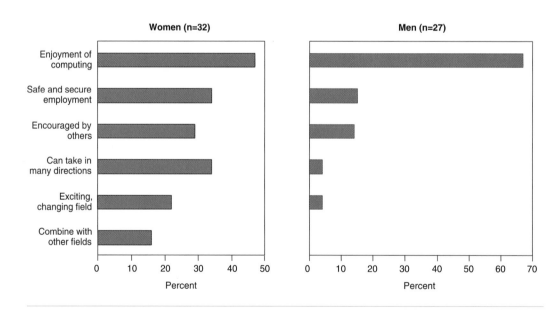

FIGURE 8 Interest in computing: Reason for majoring in computer science.

we may be able to keep this young field growing, one which enjoys the contributions of the best minds, to provide the best solutions that computing can offer.

References

Camp, T. "CS Programs in Engineering Colleges—Fewer Females," Journal of Women and Minorities in Science and Engineering, vol. 4, no. 1, pp. 15-25, 1998.

Fisher, A., J. Margolis, and F. Miller. "Undergraduate women in computer science: experience, motivation and culture," in ACM SIGCSE Technical Symposium, February 1997.

Lilian Shiao-Yen Wu
Consultant to Corporate Technical
Strategy Development, IBM
President's Committee of Advisors on
Science and Technology

WOMEN IN INFORMATION TECHNOLOGY:
A VIEW FROM INDUSTRY

I would like to give my thanks to two people. One is Jong-on Hahm who is the director of the Committee on Women in Science and Engineering; she has been invaluable in bringing together data and research in this area. The other person is my husband, Ralph Gomory. He has been my partner in my work on women. Today's talk in many ways is jointly ours.

My characterization of how women are doing in information technology and computer science in industry is that there is good news and bad news. In the previous presentation describing the declining percentage of women obtaining computer science degrees, Dr. Bill Wulf has given you the bad news that the percent of women receiving computer science B.S. degrees has been falling, and the percentage receiving M.S. and Ph.D. degrees has remained essentially around 25 percent and 15 percent. Also, during the very important K-12 period, a recent study by the American Association of

University Women shows that there is already a technology gap where fewer high school girls take advanced computer programming classes. They enter the classroom with less prior experience with computers than boys, and they are not as confident about their technology skills.

The good news is that the information technology or IT world is a terrific place for women. There are a large number of careers in IT that women both enjoy and are very good at. There are careers that are about going deeply into how the computer works, but there are also careers which involve understanding how computers can be used in innovative ways to touch our lives.

There are a number of reasons for the lower numbers of women. I will touch on two. First is what is taught. Many of the courses that a student would take to get a computer science degree are centered around the computer itself, its hardware, its operating systems, or how a compiler operates. It is not about using a computer to affect people's lives. This lack, for some women, makes computer science less attractive than other careers.

The second reason for the low numbers can be seen if we look at individuals who are successful in computers—they are portrayed in the media as nerds and geeks, people who are obsessive about getting the computer to do intricate things they want. This is not a particularly attractive role model for young girls. As a consequence, fewer girls aspire to be in computing, too many shy away from computers, and they think that because they are not nerds they are not as good at computers as boys. We then have fewer women with computer science degrees.

Now for the good news. There are two parts. The first is, despite their small numbers, women have made many fundamental contributions to the science of computers. I will briefly describe the contributions of four women: Brenda Baker and Margaret Wright from Lucent, and Fran Allen and Diane Pozefsky from IBM.

Brenda Baker has contributed to the science of computing in analysis of algorithms. She has discovered techniques for efficiently computing approximate solutions to NP-complete problems (i.e., problems that are extremely difficult to solve exactly) involving planar graphs, scheduling, and other areas of combinatorial optimization, and she has invented efficient algorithms for use in routing wires on chips, guiding robots, and finding duplication or patterns in text and software.

Margaret Wright has contributed to the science of computing through algorithms and software for numerical optimization. She has invented, theoretically analyzed, and implemented original algorithms for nonlinearly constrained optimization, including widely used sequential quadratic programming methods, and more recently, direct search and interior-point methods.

Fran Allen co-invented the framework, which has been the scientific basis for all optimizing compilers. She perceived the need to determine at compile-time how values flow through a computer program. Her paper with John Cocke, "A Catalogue of Optimizing Transformations," codified for the first time techniques that could be used to improve the running times of programs written in different computer languages and for different machines. These are still the transformations in use today.

In the early eighties, the networking technology then used by the majority of large corporations was designed for networks that rarely changed and were tightly managed. Driven by the introduction of mini-computers and personal computers, and newer connection capabilities that made it easier to add and move computers, Diane Pozefsky's work transformed the static networking technology to one that allowed networks to change with less administrative complexity, and to let network traffic adapt based on current traffic patterns. Her work has allowed networks to grow and provide immediate connectivity when new users and machines were added.

The second part of the good news is, I believe, that information technology in industry is turning into a good place for women. IT is becoming pervasive, more complex and intertwined with the telecommunications, media, and entertainment industries. It is in our homes and where we work.

As a consequence, there are careers both for people who care deeply about the uses of computers in our lives, as well as for those who care passionately about the science of computers themselves, and for every shade of interest in between.

The IT industry is moving extremely fast, e.g., we talk in terms of Web years which is 3 months. To invent, at this speed, requires working closely with customers to understand what is needed so we can find better and original approaches. Many women both enjoy and work well with customers.

A person needs some basic understanding of the capabilities and limitations of the technology but the challenge is often in being very creative in using the technology. This often involves bringing together engineers, design artists, people in IT, people who run networks, and business professionals who know the application.

One example is an IBM project that created the Internet trading operations for Charles Schwab. E-Schwab is now the largest U.S. online and discount broker. This web site regularly gets 30 million hits a day and has gotten as high as 55 million hits in one day. A project like this starts by getting the infrastructure, architecture, and technology right, including areas such as privacy and security. But just as important is to understand the customer's needs so that the application is what is really wanted and is easy to use. This requires working with and understanding business professionals and their needs.

Another example is one I have worked on. In the newly deregulated electricity industry, utilities are changing their way of doing business from a monopoly to an open market where consumers can choose who will supply their power. As monopolies, utilities dealt primarily with the engineering problem of supplying electricity in an area without interruption. But in today's open market, a utility must be concerned with other companies selling cheaper power to its customers. In this world, I have had to work not only with power engineers, but also with Wall Street traders and quants, so that the capabilities of the physical network to provide power and the optimal pricing of that power connect. My observation is that many women both find this type of work interesting and rewarding, and are good at finding inventive solutions.

Often more creative and daring ideas and solutions happen when people with different backgrounds and experiences work together on problems. I would like to illustrate this through a few examples coming from IBM's Research Division and the Women & Technology Institute, which is a nonprofit that works on technology designed for women by women. One IBM design was a small handheld device where an icon would appear if an out-of-town friend was within "being able to get together for dinner" distance. You could then send e-mail or call the friend by poking at the icon. Another design was a handheld device so that a child could add to mom's shopping list. An idea from the Women & Technology Institute was a very large video conferencing screen that could be put on the dining room wall. Then a family could have Thanksgiving dinner with other family members across the country.

All of these are examples of what I would call "person-to-person technology." They all have a bigger interpersonal component than the technology of today.

Companies appreciate the benefit of this different point of view. This together with women's ability to work with customers and in groups helps produce an atmosphere in industry that is often one of genuine support.

Before I close, I would like to mention that I believe the public rankings of companies on where they stand in areas important to women have also played an important role to advance women in industry. For example, each year companies are ranked on their family and child support policies by publications such as *Working Woman*, and the nonprofit organization Catalyst publishes the number of women on company boards. These rankings help hold companies accountable and true to their words.

In closing, my message is that a curriculum centered around technical understanding of the computer and computer software pushes away too many girls and women, although it does not push away some women who remain involved and excel. But many careers in information technology in industry are centered around the uses of information technologies. They involve both technical knowledge and the ability to work in groups with people from a variety of professions. Many women enjoy this work and do well.

I believe recognizing this, publicizing these careers, and adding courses which better reflect the broad possibilities in this industry will be interesting to more girls and women, and will better prepare them for a successful career in industry.

Plenary Panel III:

Strategies and Policies to Recruit, Retain, and Advance Women Scientists

Marye Anne Fox (Moderator)
Chancellor, North Carolina State University

SPEAKER INTRODUCTIONS

Our third panel is a round-table discussion on the barriers to recruiting, retaining, and advancing women, with Professors Howard Georgi, Karen Uhlenbeck, and Mildred Dresselhaus.

Dr. Howard Georgi is the Mallinckrodt Professor of Physics at Harvard University. He received his degree in physics from Yale in 1971, and joined the Harvard faculty in 1976, where he has served as department chair from 1991 to 1994.

Dr. Georgi has been an editor of *Physics Letters B* since 1982. His work in particle theory has involved all aspects of the standard model, particularly QCD and the grand unified theories. He and Sheldon Glassow first constructed the latter in 1973, although they are not responsible for the name. Much of Dr. Georgi's research has been in collaboration with graduate students, 39 of whom have received Ph.D.s under his direction.

Dr. Georgi is a fellow of the American

Academy of Arts and Sciences and the American Physical Society. In 1995, he received the Sakurai Prize of the American Physical Society for his pioneering contributions to the unification of strong and electro-weak interactions and for his application of quantum chromodynamics to the properties and interactions of hedrons. He was elected to the National Academy of Sciences and has written over 200 research articles and three books.

Professor Karen Uhlenbeck is Professor and Sid W. Richardson Foundation Regent's Chair in Mathematics at the University of Texas at Austin. Since receiving her Ph.D. at Brandeis University in 1968, she has also taught at MIT, the University of California at Berkeley, the University of Illinois, and the University of Chicago. She has held visiting positions at IHES in France, the University of California at San Diego, the Max Planck Institute, Harvard University, the Mathematical Sciences Research Institute, Northwestern University, and the Institute for Advanced Study at Princeton.

Dr. Uhlenbeck has been a Sloan Fellow and a MacArthur Award Fellow. Memberships include the American Academy of Arts and Sciences and the National Academy of Sciences.

Dr. Uhlenbeck has written extensively in the fields of gauge field theory and geometric calculus of variations. Her current research interests are in integral systems and geometric evolution equations. Her present activities include involvement with the IAS Park City Mathematics Institute, a mentoring program for women in mathematics. As her former colleague, I can tell you she is a force at the University of Texas for including women in the College of Natural Sciences.

Our third panelist is Dr. Mildred Dresselhaus. Dr. Dresselhaus is Institute Professor at Massachusetts Institute of Technology. She received her undergraduate education at Hunter College in New York City and her Ph.D. at the University of Chicago. Following her doctoral studies, Dr. Dresselhaus spent 2 years at Cornell as an NSF postdoc and then 7 years as a staff member at the MIT Lincoln Laboratory in the Solid State Physics Division. She joined the MIT faculty in the Department of Electrical Engineering and Computer Science in 1967, and the Department of Physics in 1983. She was named Institute Professor in 1985.

Dr. Dresselhaus is a member of the National Academy of Sciences, the National Academy of Engineering, the American Philosophical Society and is a fellow of the American Academy of Arts and Sciences, the American Physical Society, the IEEE, the Materials Research Society, the Society of Women Engineers, and the American Association for the Advancement of Science. She has served as President of the American Association for the Advancement of Science as well as numerous advisory committees and councils. She has received numerous awards including the National Medal of Science and 15 honorary doctorate degrees.

Dr. Dresselhaus is the coauthor of three books on carbon science. Her research interests are in experimental solid state physics, particularly in carbon-related materials and their intercalation compounds, and in low dimensional thermoelectrics. Her most recent interests have been in fullerenes and fullerene-related carbon nanotubes.

This panel will focus on strategies and policies to recruit, retain, and advance women scientists.

Howard Georgi, Mallinckrodt Professor of Physics

Harvard University

A TENTATIVE THEORY OF UNCONSCIOUS DISCRIMINATION AGAINST WOMEN IN SCIENCE

I will talk today about the issue of "unconscious discrimination" against women in science. I am delighted that the MIT Faculty Newsletter has brought attention to this problem. Today, I want to suggest a tentative theory of unconscious discrimination. In the light of this theory, I will discuss some possible strategies for improving things. Let me admit, at the outset, that while I have struggled with some of the issues I will discuss today for many years, I am not an expert. This is a personal attempt to understand the troubling fact of gender discrimination that I see in science.

"Discrimination" is an interesting word. There are two kinds of meanings: positives that describe the mental process of differentiation, discernment or judgment; and negatives that describe the misuse of differentiation to treat unfairly those who are different. My simplistic theory is that in unconscious discrimination against women in science, the latter follows from the former. I will argue that unconscious discrimination arises because the application of our tools for discrimination between different scientists selects for many things, including qualities, that are at best very indirectly related to being a good scientist, and that clash with cultural pressures.

In particular, our selection procedures tend to select not only for talents that are directly relevant to success in science, but also for assertiveness and single-mindedness. This causes problems for women (and others as well). There are probably other gender-linked traits that we also select for, but I will focus on these two because I think that they are particularly obvious and damaging.

I will try to explain this theory by asking and answering a number of questions.

1. Do we really select for assertiveness and single-mindedness? This question hardly needs an answer. There are many obvious examples of situations in which this selection is almost explicit. One of my favorite examples is the Physics GRE exam. I can expand on this if necessary. It is not impossible to succeed as a scientist without being assertive and single-minded, but the system encourages and rewards people with these traits in a number of ways.

2. How does selection for assertiveness and single-mindedness differentially affect women? Why should this matter more for women than for men? I realize that I am treading on dangerous ground here. Obviously, for these traits, as for any other similar traits, there is a broad distribution in both men and women, and the distributions overlap. Nevertheless, the distributions of assertiveness and single-mindedness are strongly skewed toward men. I think that most people would agree that there are very strong cultural biases that make it more difficult for women than for men to be assertive and single-minded.

3. Isn't this a problem in academia in general? Why is it worse in science? I think that the answer is that in science, we actually do have quantitative tools. There are quantitative ways of distinguishing good science from bad science, and for training good scientists. These tools really exist and they work! We produce people who do great science. This system has been honed over many years to the point that we now tend to take it for granted. It is this very success that makes it possible to accept the system uncritically, and that makes unconscious discrimination easy. I hasten to add, however, that just because we have a system that produces good scientists does not mean that the system is not eliminating many others who could be equally good.

4. Are assertiveness and single-mindedness really necessary (or even desirable) for a scientist? This question is harder. I am not sure that any controlled experiments have been done. My personal view is that what we want in a scientist is not assertiveness, but intellectual curiosity and thoughtfulness, and not single-mindedness, but dedication and perseverance. For the moment, I hope that you will accept this as a working hypothesis.

5. If assertiveness and single-mindedness are not really what we want, why did the system develop to select for these, rather than what we are really interested in? This is a question for historians and sociologists of science. But my suspicion is that the answer here has two parts. The system could develop because when it developed, there was overt discrimination against women, and so there was no selective pressure to develop a system that worked for women as well as men. It actually did develop, I think, and persists, because assertiveness and single-mindedness are easier to measure quantitatively than the qualities that we are really interested in, intellectual curiosity, dedication, and so on, which have more human dimensions. Assertiveness and single-mindedness are stand-ins that worked pretty well for a large group of men in previous generations. Even though they are no longer very appropriate, our system still selects for them. And because it "works" (at least if you ignore gender discrimination and such things), we haven't tried very hard to do better!

6. How does the selection for assertiveness and single-mindedness give rise to unconscious discrimination against women? Here there are many answers. From the top down, when department chairs and search committees look for the best scientists, they tend to exclude those who are not demonstrably assertive and single-minded. This tends to eliminate women.

   In fact, the situation is worse, because the cultural bias against assertiveness in women puts even those women who are selected by the system at a disadvantage. They may be perceived as good scientists, but disagreeable people. From the bottom up, the mismatch between the cultural stereotypes of women and scientists make it harder for girls to develop as scientists. They are constantly pushed toward other vocations. I hope that this is changing, but if so, the process has been very slow. This contributes to the familiar pipeline problem that we have already heard about today. There are not as many women as men in the pool, at any level, and the disparity increases as we go up the academic ladder. Those of us who are committed to increasing the participation of women in science find these pipeline issues incredibly frustrating. The small number of women in the pipeline makes it much more difficult to counteract the effects of unconscious discrimination in hiring. We have to convince search committees to work hard twice, both to overcome their preconception that good scientists must be assertive and single-minded, and also to identify women from a smaller pool.

7. What can be done about this? The good news is that the system is not evil, just misguided. But the bad news is that unconscious discrimination arises as a result of deep-seated habits that will be very hard to change. We have heard about some of the ideas for changing this from the bottom up. I hope that we can do it by changing our system of educating and evaluating scientists, rather than simply encouraging girls and women to break out of the cultural stereotypes against assertiveness and single-

mindedness. But meanwhile, we should try to support women's sports programs, and other things that help break down these stereotypes. From the top down, there are a few strategies that may help in hiring. The idea, in each case, is to try to open up the search procedure and make it easier to break out of the same old system.

- Do not make a single ordered list of candidates. Make several lists using different criteria. This may help remind the search committee that many talents are important to success in science, and that different candidates will rate differently in each one. Try to think carefully about all the different ways that candidates can contribute.
- Do not define the area of the search too narrowly. Very narrow searches tend to exclude women just because of pipeline issues. And the more narrow the search, the easier it is to fall into the trap of making a single-ordered list without thinking carefully about the criteria.
- Open up the search procedure. Don't let it be handled exclusively by a small committee of "experts."
- If you send a search letter, ask your informants to list the best women and minorities in the field, even if they do not rate them as highly as the top men. This will at least get people thinking about the issue, and may turn up candidates that otherwise would be overlooked.
- And most important, keep trying even when none of the strategies work. This is a job for optimists!

Karen Uhlenbeck, Professor of Mathematics
University of Texas at Austin

THE MENTORING PROGRAM
FOR WOMEN IN MATHEMATICS

The statistics for women in mathematics are particularly disturbing, since a majority of high school teachers of mathematics are women, and mathematics departments throughout the country are increasingly dependent on adjunct faculty, many of whom are women, to cover undergraduate teaching. The number of women in tenured or tenure-track positions in leading mathematics departments are few, and we are worried that this number might be decreasing. At some schools, half the undergraduate mathematics majors are female although this statistic is variable. There are a number of national programs that target undergraduate women mathematics majors, but I am aware of only two or three that include either graduate or postdoctoral level mathematicians.

Description

The *Mentoring Program for Women in Mathematics* is a 10-day program, held every year in either May or June at the Institute for Advanced Study in Princeton, New Jersey. It is connected with the Institute for Advanced Study/Park City Mathematics Institute, which runs a vertically integrated summer program for high school and college teachers, undergraduate and graduate mathematics students, and research mathematicians. The topic of the *Women's Program* is the topic of the summer school, which rotates from year to year among key areas of research mathematics. Undergraduate, graduate, and postdoctoral level women students who are accepted into the summer program receive an automatic invitation to the *Mentoring Program.* We also invite and accept applications for our program alone, but Park City students receive first priority. The number of official participants has ranged from 15 to an expected number of 40 this year. All activities are open to the public; hence the total audience for courses and seminars is much larger and includes members of the Institute for Advanced Study, Princeton graduate students, and many women visitors from local universities.

The program revolves around four activities. Two 10-day courses, one at an undergraduate level and one at an advanced graduate level, are offered. These are taught by well-known women research mathematicians in the specialty of the research area, who volunteer their time. A research-level seminar serves as a forum for advanced graduate students and research mathematicians, and a Women-in-Science seminar offers participants an opportunity to discuss readings, ask personal questions,

listen to invited panelists, and learn more about both the breadth and limitations of the mathematics community. Problem sessions and working groups on special areas more than take up any extra time. The emphasis is scientific, but intellectual and personal discussions are encouraged. Women mathematicians at the different levels are expected to interact with each other and with the local Princeton mathematics community.

History

The Park City Mathematics Institute (IAS/PCMI) came about when a group of research mathematicians, who believed that the research community should be involved in educational issues, responded to a prospectus for vertical integration, specifically in geometry, put out by the National Science Foundation (1991). Originally a group of five mathematics departments was involved, but, with great relief, the founders turned the *Park City Program* over to the Institute for Advanced Study, which under the direction of Phillip Griffiths has provided financial, staff, and intellectual support since the fourth year (1994). This next summer will be the ninth year of the summer school. I was a founding member and organized, together with my colleague Dan Freed, the first research seminar and graduate school.

I have been monitoring the participation of women closely. The large number of women high school teachers has been an embarrassing contrast to the few women researchers available. However, in our second year (1992), we ended up with an all-male group of upper-level undergraduates, and it became clear that our recruiting needed to improve. This was following by an equally embarrassing lack of women in the field of algebraic geometry in the third year (1993). The first women's program, organized by Herb Clemens, Lenore Blum, and Antonella Grassi, was held at the Mathematical Sciences Research Institute at Berkeley in 1993 with a more informal structure than the one we have now. The program was moved to the Institute for Advanced Study the following year with a more formal program and together with my coworker, Professor Chuu-Lian Terng of Northeastern University, we have been organizing it ever since. We are assisted by a group of women mathematicians from the New York-Philadelphia area. We meet with them for a discussion and lunch a couple of times a year. Some of the panels are organized by this group, and most individuals in this local program committee attend part of the program. Two permanent members of the Institute for Advanced Study, Luis Caffarelli (now at the University of Texas at Austin) and Robert MacPherson, have served as principal investigators on our grants and have lent their support to this project.

Funding

The primary funding has come from the National Science Foundation, with generous contributions from the Institute for Advanced Study and minor support from the endowment of the Regents Chair Number Three of the Sid W. Richardson Foundation in Texas. We have lost our NSF funding for future years, but hope to keep the program going with the support of the Institute for Advanced Study and its

Director, Phillip Griffiths. The formal budget for the first few years, which did not include staff support from IAS, was $30,000. However, the program has grown, and we are budgeting $53,000 for May 1999.

Goals

The original goal was to increase the numbers, preparation, and visibility of women mathematicians who apply to and attend the IAS/PCMI summer institute, and without a doubt we have succeeded. A second goal is to introduce young women to the informal network of the research mathematics community and the active sub-network among women. We try to keep participants in touch with each other through e-mail, Web pages, a reunion at the winter Joint Mathematics Meetings, and visits to the program in later years. We provide a little extra mathematics preparation and encouragement, but we also provide an opportunity for women students to hear lectures by women and to work with other women in a center of research activity.

The needs of our groups of women mathematicians are quite diverse. Some need only to see that successful women mathematicians exist; some wish to make close contact with women in their peer group; some want to help younger women students; and a few want close ties with an older mentor. The *Women's Program* meets most of these needs with a formal scientific program and lots of opportunities to meet people and carry on discussions.

The interaction between our women participants and the primarily male atmosphere at the Institute for Advanced Study has successfully influenced both sides. Many of the young women have felt more at home in Princeton because of the program, but more important, Institute members have had an opportunity to interact with talented, ambitious, and outgoing women mathematicians. It is important to introduce women to, and have them feel at home in, established scientific centers. Perhaps even more important is to actively demonstrate to both older and younger mathematicians who are in residence at IAS that there is a cadre of excellent women mathematicians, some of whom are learning the subject and some of whom are doing excellent research. Lectures and seminars are attended by Princeton graduate students and members at IAS. Changes in both atmosphere and preconceptions on both sides are noticeable.

Finally, we try to offer particularly for undergraduate students a number of ways to explore the connections between abstract mathematics and the rest of science. Standard undergraduate mathematics programs give very little of the scope of mathematics, or of the possibilities in the field. The undergraduate course in May will be on number theory and cryptography, and we try to have women visitors from both academia and industry.

Success

The program is a success, in that the number of women who go to the summer school has increased and our participants tend to rate the program highly. Even when the participants come with no recognized need for "a women's program," they are delighted to be able to air their uncertainties, see women lecturers in action, and work closely with women friends. For some, it is a first experience in the elite intellectual world of Albert Einstein, Robert Oppenheimer, and Kurt Gödel. Others simply use their entree into IAS to further their careers. However, in looking for long-term effects of the sort the scientific community values, I see our students moving up from undergraduate to graduate, picking out and using whatever mentors they found in the system, and coming back at a later stage, as graduate students or as junior mentors. And one should not discount the effect on the senior women mathematicians, invited to lecture. Senior women really enjoy the otherwise unobtainable experience of having an enthusiastic group of young women in the audience. We also are influenced to think of IAS as a less formidable and more comfortable place to take a sabbatical. I know this holds for me, and I have been told the same by other senior lecturers. The Institute community accepts and seems to welcome the eager and enthusiastic group of women each year. One has the hope that doors are being unlocked from both sides.

However, the bottom line will be to see whether through these efforts more women become mathematics professors or leaders of industrial research groups. Moreover, we hope to see more women mathematicians as members of IAS. These are long-term goals, which we might begin to assess in five or ten years.

Conclusion

Recently, while on a visit to Indiana University's Women in Science Program, I was asked by a male professor, "What should we do to encourage middle school girls?" I answered without hesitation, "Young girls are not stupid; make life easier for them when they get to be thirty." Women never ask this question, as we are as a whole very sensitive to the fact that young women need to do more math so they will end up with better jobs. But deep down there is disappointment that so little concern is expressed over the women (and men, for that matter) who are lost to the academic and research community in and after graduate school. It is rough for women, and we suspect the young girls know this. It is not clear that the scientists who are surviving into leadership are necessarily suited to develop a healthy climate for science in the next millennium. Recall that André Weil, the famous mathematician who was so influential in mathematics during this century, discusses in his autobiography his interest in Indian poetry and culture that lead him to take a postdoctoral position in India.[1] This does not fit at all into today's narrow expectations for young mathematicians. It seems obvious that we should be encouraging intellectual breadth, cooperation, and outreach along with the traditional male values of single-mindedness, competition, and confrontation. What is happening now is not necessarily for the best.

People in power, like Phillip Griffiths as head of the Institute for Advanced Study, do have the ability to foster change. For every one Phillip Griffiths, there are probably ten of me, willing to do the bits of work, but unable or not powerful or brave enough to mount a serious

challenge to the attitudes of the science community. Our program works because the Institute for Advanced Study, its Director Phillip Griffiths, the staff assigned to us, and permanent members Luis Caffarelli and Robert MacPherson, and an enthusiastic group of area women mathematicians have supported it, have helped it through political processes, and made it relatively easy to keep functioning at the highest scientific level. This is one arena in which the support of at least five members of the National Academy of Sciences has helped open locked doors for the next generation.

More information about the IAS/Park Mathematics Institute summer school and the *Women's Mentoring Program* can be found at the Institute for Advanced Study's website: http://www2.admin.ias.edu/ma/park.htm

Schedule

- 9:30 Undergraduate Lecture
- 10:45 Graduate Lecture
- 12:00 Lunch
- 1:15 Problem Sessions
- 2:30 Research Seminar and Project Groups
- 3:30 Tea
- 4:00 Open Slot
- 5:00 Women and Science Seminar
- 6:30 Dinner

Committee Members

Ingrid Daubechies, Princeton U
Irene Gamba, Courant Institute, now U Texas
Fan Chung Graham, U of Penn and UCSD
Antonella Grassi, U of Penn
Sarah Greenberg, Graduate Student, U Penn

---

[1] Varadarajan, V.S. The Apprenticeship of a Mathematician—Autobiography of André Weil (book review). Notices of the AMS 46(4): 448-456.

Nancy Hingston, Trenton State C
Rhonda Hughes, Bryn Mawr C
Jane Cronin Scanlon, Rutgers U
Diane Souvaine, Rutgers U, now Tufts
Lisa Traynor, Bryn Mawr C

Mentoring Program For Women in Mathematics

The Institute for Advanced Study, Princeton

Ten Day Scientific Program in Mathematics for:

- Undergraduate Students
- Graduate Students
- Postdoctoral-Level Mentors
- Senior-Level Lecturers and Organizers
- Panelists and Visitors

Women in Science Seminar Selected Topics

- Biographical Readings on Women
  Mathematicians

- College Teaching as a Career (Panel
  discussion)
- Working in Industry (Panel discussion)
- Women of Color in Mathematics
- Interviews with Visiting Senior
  Mathematicians
- Women Scientists and Feminism
- Best and Worst Classroom Experiences
- How Does Culture Influence Mathematicians?

Organizers

Chuu-Lian Terng, Northeastern U
Karen Uhlenbeck, U Texas

Principal Investigators

Luis Caffarelli, IAS, now U Texas
Robert MacPherson, IAS

Mildred Dresselhaus, Institute Professor
Massachusetts Institute of Technology

STRATEGIES AND POLICIES TO RECRUIT, RETAIN, AND ADVANCE WOMEN SCIENTISTS

I was asked to speak to the MIT experience on strategies to recruit, retain, and advance women scientists, because this is a topic I know something about, and because MIT represents one end of the spectrum regarding this issue. Since MIT is about 90 percent science and engineering, women students coming to MIT already have a commitment to science and engineering. During my tenure at MIT, the percentage of women undergraduates increased from 4 percent in 1967 to 40 percent today. Women graduate students have increased from 2 to 3 percent to 25 percent, and the women faculty from about 1 percent to 10 percent, the increase being an order of magnitude in each category. Present figures clearly indicate a strong interest among women to have significant careers in science and engineering. Analysis of these data over the years have shown that when the number of women exceeds 15 percent (at which point there is, on average, more than one in a recitation section), the academic performance of women students becomes equal to that of men. Over the years, the self-confidence and professional aspirations of the women have grown steadily, reaching a level today well beyond my own projections of the late 1960s.

Several factors contributed to these achievements, including a strong commitment of the MIT presidents, strong support from top MIT administrators (e.g., deans), and the leadership and hard work of women (and also men) faculty, who worked with the students, mentored them, and developed a quantitative methodology that has served us well over the years.

This methodology involves identification of an area where women have not had equal opportunity (such as athletics, housing, and so forth), work with the administration to make the relevant data available, and make recommendations for solving the problem. Variants of this methodology have been used for over 30 years to improve the status of women students. The focus on teamwork and cooperation, among the MIT women's community and with the MIT administration, has helped us accomplish a lot, with minimal trauma.

Despite the many accomplishments, we still have a long way to go. Increasing the number of women in science was necessary, but as we learned from the recent report on women faculty in the MIT School of Science, this is not enough. Issues concerning the quality of professional life of women faculty are not necessarily addressed without diligence and occasional intervention. Included in quality-of-professional life issues are salary, laboratory space, teaching assignments, service on key departmental committees, inclusion in group-funded projects, access to secretarial and technical support, and so forth. The process of collecting data to assess the quality of life of the women faculty brought women in the School of Science together and helped us understand our personal and collective situations better. The assembled data provided the MIT administration with a clearer picture on how to improve faculty career development procedures.

To address specific inequities uncovered by the report process, appropriate adjustments were made, largely through the leadership of the Dean of Science. These adjustments led to increased (documented) productivity of the women faculty, so that the small investments made by the Dean led to significant benefits to the individuals and to MIT as a whole. Similar initiatives are now under way in other schools at MIT, and the expectations are that a similar quantitative fact-finding approach involving women and men faculty and others will reveal inequities that will be amicably resolved for the mutual benefit to the faculty members and MIT as a whole.

Because of the wide press and media coverage of the MIT report, the strong endorsement by President and Mrs. Clinton for the process, and for the broad replication of the MIT approach in workplaces around the country, there is now an opportunity to make a real difference in the status of women in science and technology in academia, industry, and government laboratories. Encouragement by professional societies, private foundations, and funding agencies can help to make the replication process at other institutions a reality.

Plenary Panel IV:

Advancing Women Into Science Leadership

Marye Anne Fox (Moderator)
Chancellor, North Carolina State University

SPEAKER INTRODUCTION

Our last contribution in the symposium is from Dr. M.R.C. Greenwood, the Chancellor of the University of California at Santa Cruz, a position she has held since July 1996.

As Chief Executive Officer, Chancellor Greenwood oversees a comprehensive teaching and research institution with combined undergraduate and graduate enrollment of approximately 11,000 matriculated students and an annual budget of $265 million. In addition to her position as Chancellor, Dr. Greenwood also holds a UCSC appointment as professor of biology.

From 1993 to 1995, Dr. Greenwood held an appointment as Associate Director for Science at the Office of Science and Technology Policy in the Executive Office of the President of the United States. In that position, she supervised the Science Division providing authoritative advice on a broad array of scientific areas in support of the President's objectives.

Chancellor Greenwood is the past president of the American Association for the Advancement of Science, a member of the National Science Board, and a member of the Institute of Medicine.

M.R.C. Greenwood, Chancellor
University of California, Santa Cruz

ADVANCING WOMEN INTO
SCIENCE LEADERSHIP

It is truly a great honor to join such a distinguished and insightful group of speakers today. I want to thank Bruce and the committee for taking on the topic of women in science as part of the annual meeting of the National Academy of Sciences.

This is a first, and it should prove to be an important first for the Academy. I will be candid with you. Addressing the Academy on this issue is a challenging endeavor. Some of you know that I feel rather strongly about this topic. The strength of my convictions stem, at least in part, from the fact that I was raised as a scientist in an era that provided virtually no female role models. I did my Ph.D. at Rockefeller University where there were no tenured or tenure-track females on the faculty. There are still very few in the institution, yet in all honesty, Rockefeller provided me with a quality learning environment and mentoring environment, and an environment that built passion and challenged me to grow intellectually.

Thus, I try to be cautious about my attributions. Today, I will try to reflect on some of my own experience, but more important, I will focus on the current body of data and give you my perspective on how some of the data are changing.

Setting the Context:
Women in Business and Government

The situation for women in the biological sciences, my specific topic for today, is somewhat better than the circumstances already described in computer science, mathematics, and the physical sciences. Indeed, the landscape for women in the biological sciences for quite some time has been better than in many other disciplines. Before exploring the ascendance of women in this area, though, let me take a moment to mention the context in which we discuss these issues.

Our nation, and our world, has been struggling with the challenges of women's participation in all arenas. During the past couple of generations, and during the most recent decades, in particular, the role that women have played in our economy, our society, and our culture has evolved dramatically. Professional opportunities for women have grown from relatively low-profile and gender-stereotyped jobs to positions that involve responsibility and leadership. Women have entered and become significant contributors in many of the careers traditionally dominated by men. They now receive more than half of all baccalaureate degrees and almost half of the doctorates, own more than a third of this country's businesses, and hold tremendously influential positions in the public and private sectors.

In the federal government, for example, women are now secretaries of cabinet departments and directors of federal agencies. Our nation has a woman as Attorney General, two women on the Supreme Court, and as a reflection of the unprecedented number of women who won elective office at the national, state, and local level, the media declared 1992 "Year of the Woman." Unfortunately, some ground has been lost in some areas, but a precedent certainly has been set.

Women have entered the workforce and risen through its structure in unprecedented numbers and at a precipitous rate. While there still appears to be a durable "glass ceiling" in industry, academia, and government, the progress made by women and by the culture in professional settings is undeniable. In 1960, only about 7 percent of the nation's physicians were women. By the mid-1990s, women accounted for over 20 percent of that profession. In legal careers, the participation of women increased from about 5 percent in 1960 to about 25 percent in the mid 1990s. Positions for women in the media have also evolved such that we now find women reporting serious news, anchoring, and producing. In industry, as of 1996, nearly 8 million businesses in the U.S. were owned by women, employing over 18.5 million workers, and generating more than $2.28 trillion in sales. While women role models are still scarce in some areas, the progress already made is obvious. When I was in school these statistics and examples were unimaginable, but the female students currently in our colleges and graduate schools have been raised in a society with female role models, a society that increasingly expects talented women to set high expectations for themselves.

In addition to the readily quantifiable contributions, such as sales and profits or number and quality of publications, women have influenced the culture of business, academia, and government, and in turn, the "culture" of women has been influenced as they have taken on new roles in society. There has been a tremendous impact of professional and working women on the family, on child rearing, and on lifestyle decisions. This impact is associated with such factors as new expectations communicated to girls and young women, expectations that now include elevated aspirations for both professional and personal life.

Perhaps the greatest impact, however, has been the influence of women on attitudes and behaviors in the workplace. Men now desire and demand more family-friendly working conditions so that they may participate more fully in their families and gain the depth of experience available in their personal lives. There has been increased attention across fields and settings to the impact of interpersonal dynamics and the respect for personal rights. Team building, communications skills, and other enhancements have become focal points of lifelong learning and corporate structure, all purportedly improving productivity and creativity in the workplace.

The Ascendance of Women in Science and Higher Education

Let me spend the remainder of my time focusing on the topic of science, and under-

scoring some of the critical issues for women in my own disciplinary area, the biological sciences. Our nation's leadership in all areas of science is, in part, dependent on how well we develop our available talent pool. To remain competitive on the international front, U.S. science must attract, educate, inspire, and retain the most talented and creative individuals available. We have made progress in a number of areas, including the increase of women entering the biological sciences, but we must examine the current status and emerging trends of inclusion in the sciences to determine where further efforts are most needed.

The Importance of Developing a Strong and Diverse Talent Pool

Data reported in *Science and Engineering Indicators* (NSB, 1998) offer an unsettling picture of the emerging U.S. standing when compared to other countries (Figure 9). According to these data, in the mid-1970s the proportion of U.S. 24-year-olds earning science and engineering degrees was about 4 percent, second only to Japan, which was granting NS&E degrees to about 4.7 percent of its 24-year-olds. By the mid-1990s, although the proportion of U.S. 24-year-olds receiving NS&E degrees had increased to 5.4 percent, most countries surveyed were out-producing the U.S. proportionately. For example, the U.K. conferred NS&E degrees to 8.5 percent of its 24-year-olds, South Korea reached a proportion of 7.6 percent, Japan and Taiwan were at 6.4 percent, and 5.8 percent of Germans of this age group received NS&E degrees, to name a few. Furthermore, the modest increase in U.S. production

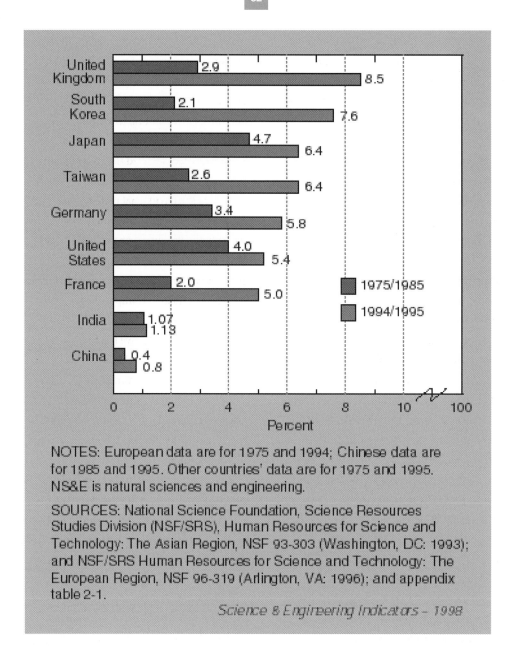

FIGURE 9 Proportion of 24-year-olds earning NS&E degrees, by country.

appears to reflect a small rise of women and minorities pursuing some areas of NS&E coupled with a small reduction in the "traditional white male student." Thus, while we are making some initial gains with underrepresented groups, we appear to be losing some of the established talent pool to other pursuits. The overall lag in U.S. student pursuit of science degrees when compared to many other nations is quite troubling, and the trends of under-representation of women and minorities in certain fields compounds the problem. To meet the challenges of the next century, we must develop a strong and diverse scientific work-force, one that has the greatest potential for developing new knowledge, pursuing innova-tion, and providing leadership.

Diversity of experience, perspective, and background can foster innovation and creativ-ity. It is clear that the participation of women, minorities, and other underrepresented groups can offer great benefits to the scientific enter-prise. There are numerous anecdotes illustrat-ing the advances in science that have occurred when diversity has entered the research enter-prise. For example, in the biological and medical sciences, the increase in attention to the likes of sickle cell, hypertension, and diabetes is often attributed to African American scientists and physicians posing new or more emphatic questions about these conditions.

Similarly, women have influenced research questions across a variety of fields. A recent anecdote from the field of neuroscience is illustrative (Figure 10). A few years ago, a study demonstrated that there are gender differences in language lateralization in the brain (see the cover story from the February 16, 1995 issue of

Nature). This study broke with tradition. That is, in neuroscience, from the time of Wilder Penfield, it has been believed that in right-handed people, language processing is lateral-ized in the left cerebral hemisphere. In the recent study, however, Sally Shaywitz (a recent IOM inductee) insisted that the experimental protocol use a sample of female undergraduates as well as the traditional male undergraduates. The result is a landmark paper showing that while language processing is indeed lateralized to the left hemisphere for most males, in the majority of females it is processed bilaterally. This has tremendous implications for under-standing brain function. It also is vital for the development of effective treatments, and suggests, for example, that men may be more resistant to certain treatments after a stroke while women's bilateral processing may offer added adaptability and treatment possibilities for overcoming deficits. Obviously, there are numerous examples of the impact women have had on the conceptualization, methodological approach, analysis, and interpretation of research endeavors. Diversity of perspectives, interests, talents, and approaches, then, can lead to vital advances in science and technology.

Biological Science Degrees Awarded to Women

The challenges faced and lessons learned in the biological sciences provide an instructive model for other sciences (Figure 11). The information available is encouraging. Currently, about 60,000 individuals receive bachelor's degrees in biological sciences each year. With more than half of these degrees being awarded to women, it appears that the interest and entry

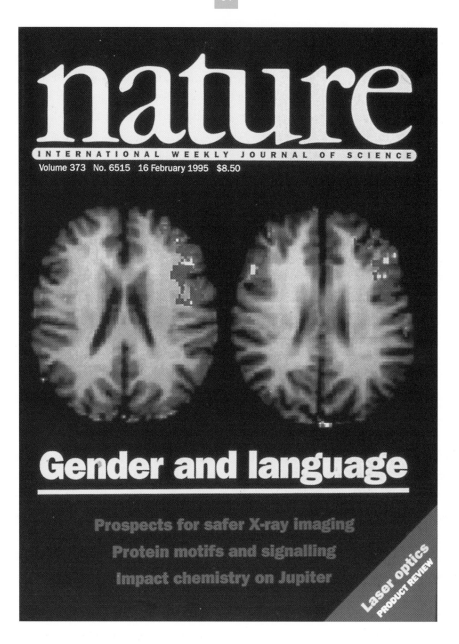

FIGURE 10 Cover of the *Nature* issue including a section on gender differences.

of women in this area is robust. Women's interest at the college level has been generally high for some time now. For example, in 1966, women received roughly one-third of these bachelor's degrees. By 1996, this figure had risen to over 50 percent.

In the Ph.D. pool, women have also shown a steady increase in their pursuit of the biological

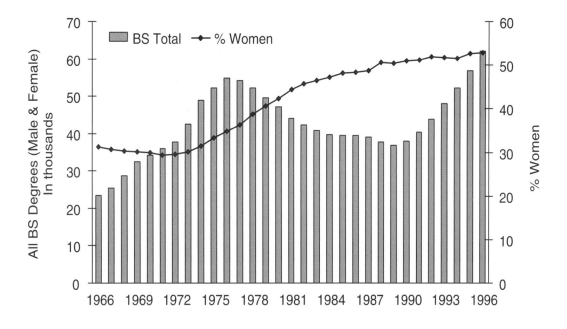

FIGURE 11 Biological sciences B.S. degrees.

sciences (Figure 12). In the mid-1960s, about 15 percent of the Ph.D.s in this disciplinary area were awarded to women. By contrast, the 1996 statistics suggest that women now receive over 40 percent of the doctorates. Thus, it is clear that women are interested in studying biological sciences, and they are demonstrating great persistence and success academically in these fields.

Women in the Biological Sciences Job Market

Entry, participation, and success at various levels of education are certainly not the only critical indexes to consider. Once women complete their education, their career options and trajectories should be examined. We need to assess what opportunities are made available,

what opportunities they pursue, and what obstacles or limitations appear to develop along the road to professional positions of leadership.

In academic careers, the trends for women in the biological sciences are quite encouraging (Figure 13). The percentage of tenured women, while still rather low, is climbing steadily. Even more promising is the rising participation of women in tenure-track positions. It is also evident that women in the biological sciences make up a large proportion of the more junior and less prestigious ranks of postdocs and "other academic" professionals, but there is no real trend here with women holding about 35 percent of these positions since about 1983 (although postdocs have grown a bit in this past year). Examining the trends of women in tenured and tenure-track positions, then, offers

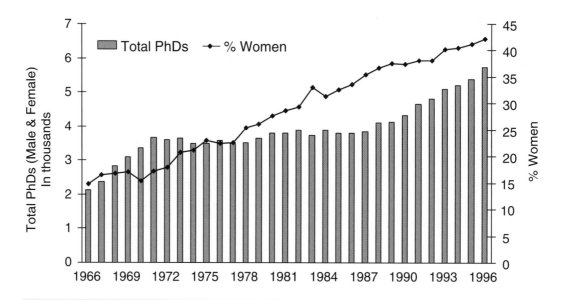

FIGURE 12 Biological sciences Ph.D.s.

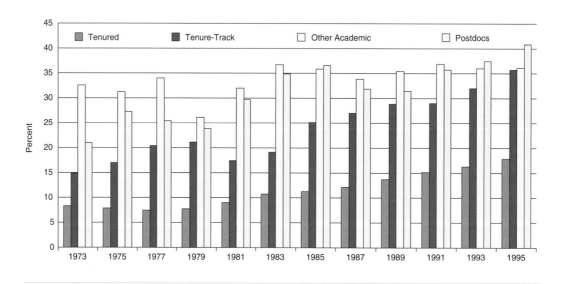

FIGURE 13 Women biological scientists in academic positions as a percentage of total (men and women).

some heartening interpretations. At first glance, it appears that there may be a significant underrepresentation of women in the higher academic ranks. The percentage of tenured women has slowly increased, from about 8 percent throughout the 1970s, to about 18 percent by 1995. While this percentage appears to be quite low, an historical analysis suggests that it is not far below expectations. That is, 10-15 years earlier, women were only about 25 percent of the pool receiving doctorates in these fields thus becoming eligible to join the faculty ranks. Perhaps most important for predictions about the future of science is the upward trend of women in tenure-track positions. This number has steadily increased, from 15 percent in 1973, to just over 35 percent in 1995. This trend appears to indicate that more and more women are poised to take leadership roles in the biological sciences.

Examining the trends among faculty, collapsed across all S&E fields, sheds additional light on the issue of women's ascent in science (Figures 14, 15, and 16). The trends are certainly not as promising as those among biological sciences, but the news is still favorable. Here again is evidence of increased participation and leadership. That is, at each rank, there is steady growth for women in academia. The number of women at the assistant professor level is not far below expectations based on past Ph.D. award rates. Specifically, the percentage of women assistant professors has increased, from just under 10 percent in 1973, to over 30 percent in 1995. One could argue that the proportion of women

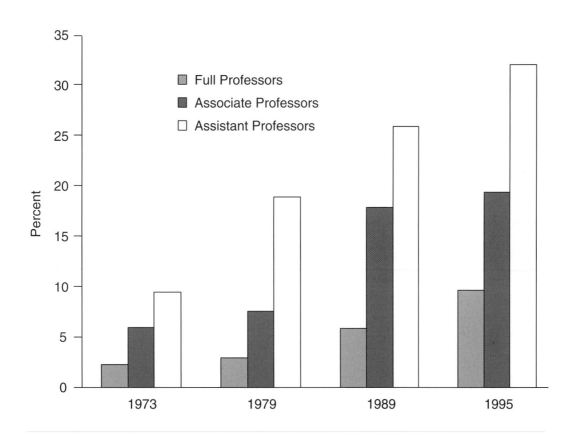

FIGURE 14 Percentage of women in faculty levels for all science and engineering.

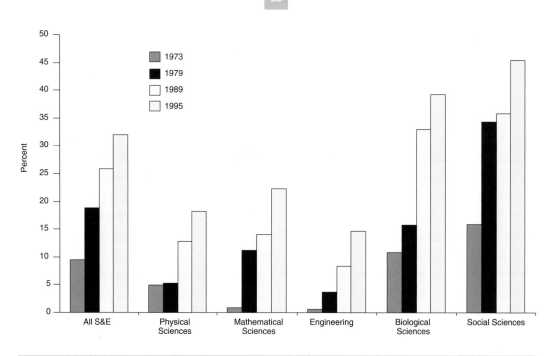

FIGURE 15 Assistant professors: Percentage of women by discipline.

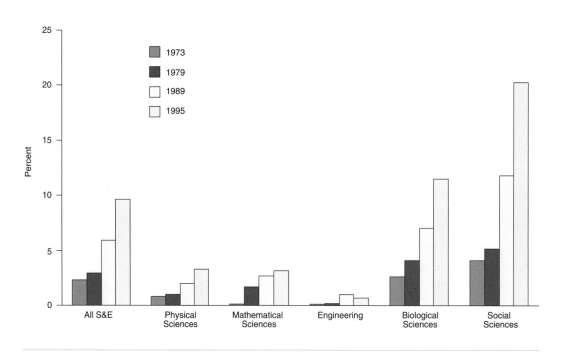

FIGURE 16 Full professors: Percentage of women by discipline.

at the associate professor level, especially in the 1990s, is also approaching the proportionate number one might expect, with increases seen from just over 5 percent in 1973 to almost 20 percent in 1995. But the data on full professors gives me pause. Overall, there is an increase in the percentage of women holding full professor positions across scientific disciplines, but the rate of increase does not keep pace with expectations. In 1973, the participation rate of women as full professors was about 2 to 3 percent, but by 1995, the numbers had not even reached 10 percent, far below the number expected given the number of doctorates awarded. That is, the percentage of science Ph.D.s awarded to women has been at, or above, 25 percent since 1970 or before. Given the number of years that it takes to move from Ph.D. to full professor, and given that much of the growth can be attributed to the increases in biological and social sciences, it appears that we may be losing a significant number of women before they reach this level. Indeed, the numbers have actually dropped in fields such as engineering, and the steady growth in physical and mathematical sciences has not yet brought the numbers of women full professors to the 5 percent mark.

Science Leadership: Representation in the NAS

If one were to try to assess the success of women in attaining positions of leadership in science, National Academy membership is a most selective measure. It has been noted that the Academy is largely comprised of male scientists. Yet, judging the Academy based on the current gender ratios in scientific disciplines

would not take into account the criteria for membership or the years of work necessary to become eligible. Instead, it seems reasonable to contrast the cohort of incoming members of the Academy with the numbers of women who received doctorates around the time that the average new members received their Ph.D.s.

The Academy provided me with some interesting data (Figure 17). In sum, the proportion of current NAS members who are women is quite similar to the percentage of science Ph.D.s awarded to women about 30 or more years ago, a time when many current members were receiving their doctorates. That is, it appears that women make up between 5 percent and 6 percent of each group. In some disciplinary areas, the percentage of women in the Academy, while still very low, seems to exceed expectations based on pre-1969 doctoral award data. Astronomy, for example, reportedly awarded about 3 percent of its Ph.D.s to women pre-1969, yet the NAS percent is above 5 percent. Genetics, on the other hand, illustrates the opposite result. Pre-1969, almost 25 percent of the doctorates were conferred on women. While currently, the NAS section has only about 17 percent women. Thus, while it might be expected that disciplines with large numbers of women would have higher rates of female membership to their NAS sections, the membership numbers are far closer to expectations once the historic data are taken into consideration.

Again, it is worth reiterating the more recent increases of women in a range of science disciplines, especially at the tenure-track and tenured level. Given these trends, one would expect women to make great gains in leadership activities and positions in upcoming years,

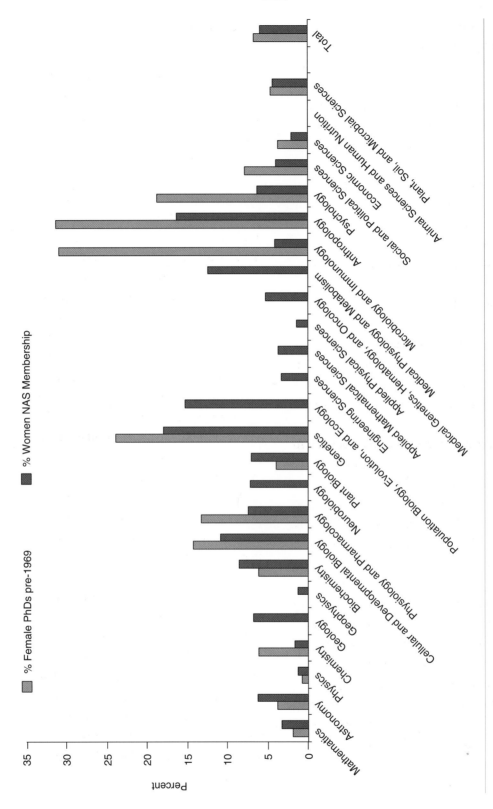

FIGURE 17 Percentage of women scientists (Ph.D.s awarded pre-1969) currently employed in Research I and II Institutions and percentage of current female NAS membership by section.

including membership to the National Academy of Sciences. There is promise that in the next 30 years there will be substantially more female leaders in many areas of science.

All of the data on education and academic employment taken together offer reason for celebration mixed with reason for concern. Certainly, there are many fields of science in which women show an enduring interest, from the time they enter college until the time they retire from long and fruitful careers. There are other areas, however, in which women seem to leak out of the pipeline, after receiving their bachelor's degrees and at many points along their career paths. Leakage from the pipeline is a costly loss of talent, especially when women leave science careers after substantial investments of time, education, funding, and other resources have been dedicated to them and by them.

The most difficult problems, in fact, may be the types of issues exposed in the MIT report already discussed today. The MIT study was so astonishing in part because it illuminated the situation for women at equal status to their male counterparts, at an undeniably elite institution, and at an institution that takes such pride in its female faculty's accomplishments and contributions. One of the most compelling findings of this study, as you have heard from other speakers today, is that the productivity of these women increased precipitously after the university took steps to correct the inequities. As has already been noted, the interventions could thus be seen as economically sound investments as indicated by such factors as the amount of additional indirect cost money that came into the institution because of the increased productivity.

Employment of Female Biological Scientists Across Sectors

Finally, it is worth examining the professional opportunities available to, and pursued by, women in the biological sciences. While there has been much talk recently of the "overproduction" of Ph.D.s, it is equally clear many talented young scientists in all demographic groups are finding nontraditional careers to be rewarding, both financially and intellectually, and they are enjoying the challenges of bringing their disciplinary knowledge to new (and possibly more appreciative) venues. This trend is already evident in the growing interest in industry jobs, and novel career paths are emerging in other sectors as well. I recently learned, for example, that the USDA is the largest single employer of veterinarians in the world. Despite the fascinating job opportunities, however, USDA is recruiting veterinarians from Southeast Asia. There are other new and emerging careers for women biological scientists in government. Positions, from state health officers to policy analysts, are opening and they seek highly trained personnel who have a depth of understanding of science coupled with an interest in societal questions and public policy.

The most common career choice for women in biological sciences is education, and as already noted, women account for an increasing percentage in this sector. In the past 20 or so years, as new opportunities have emerged in other sectors the percentage of women in industry and government has also risen (Figure 18). Specifically, the percentage of women in education has doubled from 1973 to 1995, growing from about 13 percent to about

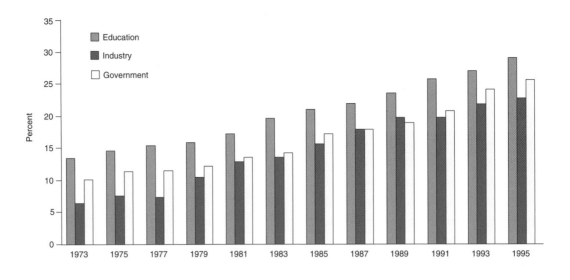

FIGURE 18 Percent of women biological scientists employed in different sectors.

28 percent, while the comparable growth in women's participation in industry has tripled from around 7 percent to near 23 percent. Similarly, women increasingly have found a home in government, with participation rates increasing substantially from about 10 percent in 1973 to just over 25 percent a couple of years ago.

One reason that women may be choosing careers in industry in increasing numbers is the clarity of corporate structure and the less ambiguous conditions of employment. In many respects, employment in industry is less mysterious than academia. Furthermore, the corporate environment has often made more accommodations to needs in such areas as family leave and child care than we have made in academia. We in academia are losing talent to other professional careers in part due to our neglect of changes in work culture.

Regardless of the new and growing interest in alternative careers, the pervasive attitude in many academic departments continues to be that the only meaningful career for graduates is a career in academia, especially tenured positions at R-1 institutions. Indeed, the pejorative and stigmatizing attitudes towards alternative careers at times seems to be intractable.

Showing True Leadership

More than half of the students attending college and receiving bachelor's degrees are now females. If we cannot secure, from that incredible pool, a cadre of talented women interested in scientific fields, then we will be left to fill our disciplines with talented students from the countries that are showing a growing interest in the sciences. As has been said so many times, one of the great assets of the

United States is our vast and diverse human resource. Rather than "weed out" students and discourage them from enrolling in science classes, we must encourage and inspire them when they are young. We must encourage their creativity and curiosity. And we must nurture their careers so that the most talented and skilled scientists emerge to lead the next generation.

We are at a crossroads in our nation. This is a time when we need the voice and guidance of leadership. Over the past few years, we have developed a new understanding and new insight into the obstacles to entry and the factors contributing to attrition of women in the sciences. We have also gained a deeper appreciation of the consequences of losing talent. The issue of women's full participation in science and engineering is no longer as it was when I first developed my interest in this topic. It is no longer a simple issue of discrimination against women. The issue has become more complex. We must now look at the interaction of factors that influence whether students are attracted to fields of science, and factors affecting whether they persist in their studies and careers rather than abandon the sciences to pursue other careers.

I hope we will reach the day when we no longer hear that the "first woman" has been elected or appointed to a coveted and influential post or made a notable contribution to a previously all-male endeavor. Science has always fueled economic growth and innovative advancements for society. Science has done this, in great part, through human creativity, innovation, collaboration, and tenacity. It is now for the science leadership to ponder and discuss how best to protect and develop the human resource to ensure a future that will benefit us all.

Marye Anne Fox (Moderator)
Chancellor, North Carolina State University

Closing
Remarks

Please join me in thanking our presenters: Dr. Leon Lederman for telling us about simplicity and complexity in learning; Dr. Richard Tapia for describing the importance of mentoring and culture, and of the value of nurturing students; Dr. Marcia Linn for teaching us how to engage in discovery as part of education; Dr. Bill Wulf for telling us about the differential aspirations that influence a young woman's decision to remain in computer science; Dr. Lilian Wu for illustrating for us how creative and interactive solutions that involve interpersonal relationships can improve women's performance in computer science; Dr. Howard Georgi for recognizing the troubling fact of unconscious gender discrimination, and showing how the emphasis on assertiveness and single-mindedness can influence academic decisions; Dr. Karen Uhlenbeck for demonstrating how private support can enhance the integration of young women into our fields; Dr. Mildred Dresselhaus for telling us how a critical mass (that is, number of participants) really can influence academic decisions and how academic leadership is important in these ideas; and finally, M.R.C. Greenwood for telling us about alternate careers and for leadership in the biological sciences.

Thanks to you all of you for being here, and thanks to the NAS Council for supporting this symposium.

Question and Answer Comments

Marye Anne Fox (Moderator)

Chancellor, North Carolina State University

PANEL I

THE NEXT GENERATION: SCIENCE

FOR ALL STUDENTS

Participant: Dr. Marcia Linn, I am very excited by the stimulation of what getting controversy in the class might do, but I would like you to contrast that observation with what struck me as an important presentation by Sheila Widnall when she was president of the AAAS. Her address was published in *Science*.

She did a little personal survey of female graduate students at MIT and asked them about their experience at MIT (and they were mostly in hard sciences), and they said, to make a long story very short, that they had no problem competing with the men in all the work in the graduate school, but they found the experience exceedingly uncomfortable because they didn't like being forced to compete in sort of Oxford high table style of put-down-the-other-person-intellectually in the classroom.

They wanted a more cooperative environment in which people's interactions in the classroom were intended to be supportive rather than confrontational. It sounds a little bit like it is a different message from the excitement born of controversy, and I wonder if you would comment on that and specifically with respect to female students?

Response: Dr. Linn: Thank you very much for asking that question. I think that is really important, and that was part of the pedagogical content knowledge that the teachers needed to work out because they wanted to provide a window on science in the making. They wanted students to be linking and connecting ideas, to be considering alternatives, and to be asking each other questions. One of the things that they worked out was a system where, for every presentation, all the students in the class needed to write a question down, and then they gave all those questions to the person who made the presentation.

So, everybody was treated the same, and everybody felt like, you know, this is part of science rather than, "Oh, my God, somebody is going to ask me a question. I won't know the answer. I don't want to take a risk," and it is also true that we encourage students to use an on-line discussion where they could participate anonymously, and both boys and girls, actually equally often chose to be anonymous.

So, I agree with you. I think actually the issue here is, as one philosopher described it, that science in the making is a seething conversation and what we want to do is to communicate the excitement of that, the fact that it is a sustained reasoning process, and that it is okay to revise and rethink your ideas. Right now that is very rare in the science classroom.

Participant: Yes, my comment is for Dr. Richard Tapia. I really appreciated your comments. As a Ph.D. student in chemistry, everything you said strongly resonated with my experience, and I think that you are correct. The missing link, in this whole equation, is the mentorship that is necessary to bring minorities and women into science, and my question is what incentives can universities put in place to make mentorship an integral part of the educational experience?

Response: Dr. Tapia: I appreciate your comments, and right now the National Science Foundation, and I am on the National Science Board, we realize that, and what we are trying to do is make the department a focal unit. At Rice, I could tell you three departments that are so-called "good" departments and three departments that are "bad" departments (and you could guess which ones they are) and I have tried to get our administration—our deans, our provost, and our president—to reward those departments for that activity. Our department, which takes a strong lead, and the individuals in that department have been very strongly rewarded.

So, they put this in alignment. In other words, the reward system is now in alignment with the mission statements that presidents often say, and so I am saying that at the National Science Foundation and within the university those departments that do good jobs, and notice as I said before, not everybody has to do the same thing, but look at the unit and say, "You will be rewarded."

We have been extremely well rewarded and treated well, and it was started by some of our deans and provosts who are in the audience here, but we have been very well rewarded and the faculty buys in to say that this is a positive thing. Look at the rewards we get. We get travel funds. We get an extra position. So, I think we have to tie it together and put it into the reward system.

Participant to Dr. Linn: I was also somewhat concerned about the feeling I was getting that science was a branch of forensics, and the hardest thing I have had to teach graduate students and postdocs is when they have written a paper and they get things from the reviewers they say, "I have to refute this." I say, "Maybe you should read it first. Maybe he or she is right," and they quite often are, and this goes on up to the very top level in science, and the newspapers always try to emphasize these controversies, when I really think if the real history of science were known, it would be people trying to explain things to one another rather than to fight with one another.

Response: Dr. Linn: Thank you very much for that question. I really agree with you. The term "controversy" is accurate because it really helps students connect to what happens in their daily lives and in the newspaper, which is, for most people, their likely source of science information after they finish science class. One of our goals is really to get students to realize that they need to rethink and reflect on their ideas. So, although we are calling this "controversy," we definitely think of it as knowledge integration and reflection, and sort of helping students understand the way controversy works, in science, is not just people shouting at each other, but actually a process where ideas are warranted with evidence, and in fact, as you saw that one student's presentation. What happens in the class is the average argument that a student makes in the debate is warranted with two pieces of evidence.

In contrast, if you look at a discussion, in a typical science class, it is much more similar to the review process that you mentioned where students just say, "No, that is wrong. Well, I think this," and so in fact, I think that what the goal here is to actually get people to engage in discussion about science that has the real evidence as part of their thoughtful process.

Participant: Thank you. I wonder where in all this, if anywhere, is there anything to do with antiscience and pseudoscience and so on. This is a considerable problem. I mean where do the children learn to discriminate or how do they learn, if at all?

Response: Dr. Linn: One of the things that we are interested in is helping students early become critics of the Internet material that they encounter, and indeed, if you want a good source of alternative medicine, actually one of my favorite Web sites now, and I will refer you all to it is astro-economics, where you can use astrology to improve your economic forecasting skills. I think that starting early with developing critical thinking skills about the Internet materials that are out there and available is really a great opportunity, and one of the things that we are trying to do in this program is present the Internet as something that needs to be viewed with some skepticism.

The most common assignment currently,

today in science class, is to go to the computer room and just look at three Web sites, but not with any information about how to be critical with regard to those Web sites. So, one of our goals is really to help students develop an inquiry process that includes thoughtful ways to look at two different pieces of evidence and try

to understand whether they fit together as well as good skills in trying to determine who posted this information, and under what circumstances should I actually believe it.

So, it seems to me that the Internet is a great opportunity for developing critical thinking.

Question and Answer Comments

Marye Anne Fox (Moderator)

Chancellor, North Carolina State University

PANEL II

AN IN-DEPTH VIEW OF COMPUTER SCIENCE

Participant: I would like to make a comment. Thank you all, thank you, both, for this interesting discussion. Those of us who can remember 40 years ago, women in science, remember that we were told that something wonderful was about to happen. New departments of computing would be formed in universities, departments that did not have a history of a male establishment, and therefore these departments would immediately be 50 percent women, 50 percent men. You have shown us very graphically that that didn't happen.

I would suggest that the decline is the result of two things. In almost every case, the organization is deep within a male academic community, and for the same reasons that the National Academy of Sciences does not have many women, these male departments do not have many women.

I think Richard Tapia was right. We need a better support system. We call it a crisis of confidence, but I think that is the wrong terminology. I think the truth is these women are not being supported in the fashion that would make it possible for them to succeed.

Therefore, I would like to make the following suggestion, that some kind of an experiment be carried out, and in view of Lilian's interesting ideas, I am even going to change what my suggestion (before she had gotten toward the end of hers) was going to be. That some department somewhere establish a computer or a subcomputer organization that has more female faculty than male, that you let people study under that environment, and see who has the crisis of confidence.

But I believe, and I think all of us who have looked at the statistics believe what Lilian said, and that is that industry has done a better job than academia in supporting women.

So, now, I wonder whether industry and perhaps even IBM could set up an academic division, in which anyone could come and teach, but again, where a significant number of the faculty are women. So, that is a question, if you want to answer.

Response: Dr. Wu: I have a reaction. About 10 years ago, right before I joined the Committee on Women in Science and Engineering, I would say that industry, at that point, wasn't so great. It was pretty much the way I would say what I hear from my colleagues in the academic world, the same kinds of problems, the same kinds of chilly atmosphere, and it has only been in the past 5 years could I really comfortably say that, you know, the atmosphere is quite different, and it has changed to be an atmosphere that is supportive.

I think there are a number of reasons for

that in IBM, but I think that the change is real, and the appreciation for what women can actually bring to technology is one that is really real.

So, I am actually quite optimistic that once all of the very, very bright people start thinking about this, and if you do come to the conclusion that it really is something that makes sense, that things will happen because it happened at IBM in my own experience very, very quickly. Once it was recognized, once it was believed that this is something good, we really changed the atmosphere around.

So, it can happen quite fast.

Response: Dr. Wulf: I think this is a fascinating idea. I was listening to Lilian and trying to map the notion of fast change onto any of the academic departments I know of.

I don't want to go there, okay?

Participant: I am compelled to say that it is 1999, and the legislation, the laws banning discrimination changed, what, 20 years ago? The number of Ph.D.s in physics and astronomy has been 10 percent for 100 years, and in the last 10 years the National Academy of Sciences has elected 2 percent women.

Things are not changing in the Academy, and I laughed at the notion of if working women, for example, are catalysts doing the survey in academia what they provide in terms of child care and maternity leave, support structures, I laugh at that notion. It would be so hysterical to see what they would find.

My experience is that, I am an academic astronomer, these universities have no interest in general. Rice is probably a small exception.

There is no interest in changing the number of women percolating up through the ranks. The statistics that are on the Web from the NSF and everywhere else show that there is leakage, and I don't even like that term "leakage" at every step of the pipeline. What it really means is ongoing discrimination. The percentage of women who are promoted to tenure is lower than their percentage in the pool. I mean the percentage of men who are promoted to tenure. They take longer to promote to tenure. There is the lovely work by Sonnert and Holton, which shows that even the top, the elite women in science, and NRC postdocs suffer from this discrimination.

It seems to me—and I will conclude this speech—I am sorry to go on, but it seems to me that there is a fundamental break between the beliefs of a traditional academic world, which believes in their souls that the best succeed and the objective evidence, which all of us as scientists should be able to evaluate, which is that the best do not succeed, that is that many of the best are not succeeding.

Participant: It is not really a question. It is a comment, and I wasn't sure whether I should make it or not, but I am a little distressed. In fact, I am quite distressed at the message that seems to be coming through that women are intrinsically less interested in how things work and how they are put together; in what I consider to be the interesting things; that they are interested really for what appear to me other reasons. I am not saying that they are periph-eral, but they are intrinsically different, and that may in fact be true. If it is true, I am really distressed to find out that it is true.

I think it is not true, and I think that the problem is really elsewhere. I don't know where it is, but I don't think that is where it is at.

Response: Dr. Wu: In the kinds of things that I have worked on, the understanding how it works is a very big part of it, as well, and it is not so much an understanding how the computer works *per se* but understanding how deregulating the electricity market would work, and there is just as much understanding *per se* in that question of what are the right kinds of regulations for the government to put down versus those that they should leave alone and let industry figure out for itself.

I think those are just as worthy questions to think deeply and passionately about, and I am not sure the computer, thinking deeply about the computer *per se* is the only thing that one can get passionate about.

Participant: Just a brief comment on process. One thing that is different about industry, at least in my industry and I think, also, at IBM, is that we have been required to address this issue face on for at least the last decade and atten-dance at consciousness–raising encounter sessions is mandatory, and we have seen a massive change in our behavior over the last decade.

Question and Answer Comments

Marye Anne Fox (Moderator)
Chancellor, North Carolina State University

PANEL III
STRATEGIES AND POLICIES TO RECRUIT, RETAIN
AND ADVANCE WOMEN SCIENTISTS

Participant: I want to thank Howard so much for introducing the issue of evaluation and, also, the MIT women's report. I certainly agree that it is the single women's faculty report that is going to help (I think), other universities take comparable steps, but I would like to bring up again the issue of evaluation. In that report, there is one wonderful sentence that says something to the effect that the whole issue after all is the role of prejudice in evaluating talent.

That is a statement from the MIT Women's Faculty Report and documenting discrimination, prejudice in the way that talent of the tenured women faculty particularly was being evaluated by their peers and their department heads, and I hope that others will agree that looking at that evaluation could move us all along.

Participant: I would like to point out just to remind us that very tough research lies ahead to understand all these issues, and I will cite a trivial example and then one that truly puzzles me. The trivial example, back to your presentation, is that in our law schools I believe the majority of law students, in the United States, are now women. I think it is even a significant majority, and yet assertiveness is surely a criterion for selection of law students. At least it wouldn't be totally inappropriate, but the other example I wanted to give is one where there is no pipeline explanation. There is no social postpuberty explanation, and it comes from the National Geographic Society's Geographic Bee. There is a competition every year; some 8,000 to 10,000 middle schools participate. The children are between the ages of 8 and 11. At the school level, when they compete in the geography bee, and there is a lot of science, let me say in geography the way it is defined, the girls and the boys do equally well.

They then go on to compete at a regional and state level. At the state level, the girls win about one-third of the time and the boys about two-thirds of the time. The winners in the states go to Washington, about 50 or 60 of them, and they have a competition to determine which 12 will appear on television for the final end.

Out of that group, typically it is 11 boys and one girl, and there was one year when that one girl won the whole thing. That was pretty impressive, but the Geographic Society cannot understand what this is all about, and they tried. If any of you want a research grant from the Education Foundation at the Geographic Society, and you have a way to figure out what is causing this issue for 8- to 11-year-old kids then they would like to know. I think it is profoundly curious.

Response: Dr. Fox: Judges.

Participant: No, it isn't. You would have to say there is gender bias in the questions—these questions are quite explicit questions that have right and wrong answers. It isn't judges.

Participant: I would like to ask a slightly narrower question that I realize puts Mildred on the spot, but I think the fascinating issue with the MIT report is the question of why this happened.

You stressed, for example, the supportive nature of the president. Why did this happen? There must have been a lot of discussion on this or at least if you would be willing to give us your personal view, I would be very interested in that.

Response: Dr. Dresselhaus: Could you clarify your questions why what happened, why there was a —

Participant: The degree of inequality in treatment of apparently very distinguished faculty in issues such as space, for example, I mean is it because, I don't know, I could hazard many guesses, but I would be interested in hearing what you think.

Response: Dr. Dresselhaus: I remember when we got together the first time, we went around the room. The first cycle was for more than half of the people present—self-denial that there was any difference, that our treatment had been different. By the time we went around the room the second time, and we heard what the others said, we said: "Oh, that happened to me, too," and so, I think a large part of the difference is that women do not ask for, they are not as aggressive in asking for equality in salaries, and equality in amenities. I speak for myself. I certainly have not done that in my career, and as I look back on my career, there were many instances where I was shortchanged, and I didn't complain. I said, "I will just work within the system."

Now, whether this has something to do with our upbringing or what, part of the problem is us. It is not all them.

Participant: I want more women to be Nobel Prize winners and to be members of the National Academy, but perhaps even more than that I want it to be possible for women to be good scientists, not just brilliant ones, just as most men are good scientists and engineers, not members of the Academy.

Balancing family issues is a difficult thing for women. Some years ago a very successful scientist came to speak at our university for Women's History Month, and as she was discussing her career she mentioned that she had taken less than four days of maternity leave for the birth of her four children.

This is the stuff of a superwoman, which is, in fact, what she is. What the men in the audience took away from that was that this was the way that women should approach having a family. What the women took away from it was that this was what the men would now expect and that this was not possible for them.

I wanted a comment from the panel because I think actually the reason this woman had told the story was that she wanted to show that it was possible to have a brilliant career and to have a family, but I think the result was not a good one and in fact, the woman who told the story is on a panel today, and so, I would like her comments on this, Dr. Dresselhaus?

Response: Dr. Dresselhaus: The question is at me, and I will try to answer it. I think that in my youth it was almost necessary to play the game that way. We didn't have so many options. However, I think there are other women who would disagree with me and would say that we should not have surrendered, and we should have behaved as we wished rather than as we thought society expected us to act.

Okay, that being the case, you will notice from my list I did not have anything on childcare and family care, and the reason for that is that we don't really have very good data on this, and I believe that we have not solved that problem very well within our community at MIT yet. I think we are working on it. That is one of the future issues. I believe that childcare is one of the critical needs for working women, not only women scientists, but all kinds of working women.

I would like to see better childcare available in general for all categories of women that is better quality and more affordable. We are not there yet. I believe that this is a responsibility of all society, not only women. It is for everybody to deal with.

Now, finally, you asked about young women. Young women don't have to endure the situation that I went through because it is much more acceptable now to have a family than it was a long time ago. However, it is not much easier, and we have to try to solve that and make it more doable. It is more acceptable, but it is not easier.

Participant: Yes, Mildred, to put you on the spot again —

Response: Dr. Dresselhaus: Okay, I am used to it.

Participant: You spoke about having a strong commitment from the president, a lot of support from the senior administration and deans, and yet MIT in case anybody else doesn't know it has zero tenured women in mathematics, and that has been the case for a long time.

Response: Dr. Dresselhaus: It is not the only department.

Participant: And it is not the only university either, but if you have got all this support, and you still have zero women. What do you do about it?

Response: Dr. Dresselhaus: What do we do about it? We talk about it. We have had a number of women who have had appointments in the department, some extremely promising. Some who had good possibilities for tenured appointments chose not to remain. Others who have been offered positions at the tenured level have chosen not to come. There are reasons for it, but you are quite right. That is a failure, and we have many failures. As I look through our statistics, we are only 10 percent or so women faculty. We have 40 percent women students. So, the pipeline is not going. Our flow chart is not without some obstructions, and we have to try to get over them.

You know a career in academia is not an easy thing today for women, and the more competitive the university, the more difficult it is, and one of the problems that we have at our institution is so many of our women students who are extremely capable are turned off from academic careers because they see it is so hard.

This is, also, true of men. It is not only a women's issue. This is a problem that we have and hopefully, we can do something to change it. I think this is a good COSEPUP topic. It is not a trivial thing.

To summarize, you have raised very important issues—that there are no tenured women in mathematics. I am hoping that within 5 years we can report that this has changed.

Participant: This is with regard to the last question, that at least at Princeton we have been able to have, in the last few years, a many-fold increase in the number of senior women in science and engineering, and I would probably not like to talk about the means in front of a microphone for fear of bringing the feds down on my head. Part of the reason, of course, is we started with such a low base, but I think it really is possible to do things that will make a big difference in this area.

Response: Dr. Dresselhaus: You had leadership at the top. You had a lot of strong support from the top.

Response: Dr. Fox: They had scientific leadership at department levels, at deans' levels, and at upper administration levels, something that I really think you need to think about as well with respect to these questions.

I can tell you it does not go without notice the fact that I can sign on a budget for $750 million a year in the administration of North Carolina State University.

That leads on to our next topic which is about advancing women into scientific leadership, and thank you again for the suggestions.